Claude Anctil
May, 1962

JOSEF PIEPER

JUSTICE

translated by

Lawrence E. Lynch

PANTHEON BOOKS

German title:
Über die Gerechtigkeit

Manufactured in the U.S.A.
American Book-Stratford Press, Inc., New York

CONTENTS

"Justice is destroyed in twofold fashion:
by the false prudence of the sage and by the
violent act of the man who possesses power."

ST. THOMAS, *On the Book of Job* [8, 1].

1. ON RIGHTS

AMONG all the things that preoccupy us today, there seem to be few that are not connected with justice in a very intimate fashion. A survey of current problems reveals this clearly. There is, first and foremost, one of the most urgent concerns of our times: How can genuine authority be once more established in the world? There are the problems of "human rights," of a "just war" and war-crimes, of responsibility in the face of unjust commands; the right of opposition against unlawful authority; capital punishment, duelling, political strikes, equality of rights for women. Every one of these issues is, as we all know, controversial. And each one has an immediate connection with the notion of justice.

Over and above that, however, anyone who judges the realities encountered in everyday life by the standard of "justice" will clearly see that evil and suffering in our world have many names, but primarily that of "injustice." "Man's greatest and most frequent troubles depend on man's injustice more than on adversity." [1] Consequently, when Aristotle undertakes to explain the distinctive and fundamental forms of justice, he expressly starts from what is our most familiar experience, and that is injustice. "The many forms of injustice make the many forms of justice quite clear," [2] he says.

All that is true, yet whenever "justice" is analyzed, so vast a multitude of meanings come to mind that it is quite impossible to master them. Nevertheless there is a notion of the utmost simplicity to which that bewildering variety can be reduced. Indeed, Plato already mentions it as if it were handed down by long tradition.[3]

It is the notion that each man is to be given what is his due.

Wherefore all just order in the world is based on this, that man give man what is his due. On the other hand, everything unjust implies that what belongs to a man is withheld or taken away from him—and, once more, not by misfortune, failure of crops, fire or earthquake, but by man.

This notion, then, the notion of the *"suum cuique,"* which ever since the very earliest times became the common possession of the Western tradition through Plato, Aristotle,[4] Cicero,[5] Ambrose,[6] Augustine [7] and, above all, through Roman law,[8] will have to be discussed in what follows. More precisely, the discussion will have to be about the intentional habit that enables man to give to each one what is his. In a word the *virtue* of justice must be investigated.

"Justice is a habit (*habitus*), whereby a man renders to each one his due with constant and perpetual will." [9]

In the essay we are now undertaking, a very special place is accorded to the author of this statement, Thomas Aquinas. Nonetheless our purpose is not to contribute a study in the history of the philosophy of the Middle Ages. Our aim is, rather, to present a model formulation of the ideal image of justice, to redevelop it as a concept, and bring it face to face with our contemporary world. In the present context we will not discuss whether or not the doctrine concerning the virtue of justice, as found in the works of St. Thomas,[10] does, in fact, provide the most *exemplary* expression of the traditional wisdom of Western morality, nor whether Thomas Aquinas does rightly bear the name "Universal Doctor" of Christendom. These points are simply taken for granted. It is our feeling that in this field originality is of scarcely any importance. The person to whom what matters is a thorough understanding will endeavor to partake of and grasp the already established true knowledge of man which is not to be set at nought by the advance and march of time. That will, of course, only be accomplished if his eyes are not just fixed on the documents of tradition but, rather, on the matter itself.

Our attention, therefore, is not focused on Thomas but, rather, on the foundation of that whole specifically human obligation implied in the proper conception of justice.

There are, of course, other definitions of justice in the Western tradition, too. In Thomas himself there are several kinds of definition each with a different ring to it. Thus, in one place he says that justice is that whereby what is one's own is distinct from what belongs to a stranger; [11] or again: it is properly the mark of justice to establish order among things.[12] Augustine has likewise spoken of the virtue of justice in many different ways. A particular luster attaches to the following formulation: "Justice is that ordering of the soul by virtue of which it comes to pass that we are no man's servant, but servants of God alone." [13] Yet such statements are hardly intended to be proper definitions of the term. That is true only of the statement already quoted—the most sober and factual of all—and which says: justice is the virtue which enables man to give to each one what is his due.

I have just said that this idea is an extremely simple one. But that does not imply that its meaning is easily grasped and, as it were, without paying any price. For what, in fact, is each man's due? And above all, what is, generally speaking, the basis for a *"suum"?* How does anything come to belong to a person, anyway? And how does it so truly belong to him that every man and every human authority has to grant it to him and allow him to keep it?

Perhaps as a consequence of what has happened throughout the world during the past decades—and is still happening—we are now newly gifted to see what is properly involved in such a fundamental consideration. The answer is no longer self-evident; the most extreme formulations—and realizations, too—of Absolute Untruth have come to the fore; and thus the deepest foundations of truth are once more called in question because they are expressly attacked. It is therefore opportune and, indeed, necessary to think these matters through in a new and more radical fashion.

"If the act of justice is to give to each man his due, then the act of justice is preceded by the act whereby something becomes his due."[14] This text expresses with supreme simplicity a circumstance that is utterly fundamental. Justice is something that comes second: Right comes before justice. If something is due to a man as his own, the fact of its being due to him has not come into existence through justice. "That act, by virtue of which something comes for the first time to be due to a man as *his*, cannot be an act of justice."[15]

Let us take an example. One man does a job for another, let us say he digs his garden for him. (For

13

the purpose of our example, we assume that in performing this task he is not fulfilling a previous obligation.) By his digging, something due to him has come into being. By reason of something that he has done, something is now due to him. And that other man must give him his due. Now this act of giving is an act of justice, and it has as its condition, then, the fact that something is due to his neighbor.

Everyone is aware, however, that there are rights which do not arise out of one's work; in other words, that man has a right to some things as his due, which has no basis in any action of his. No one, for example, doubts that a man has a right to his own life.

Now the question that arises in this connection goes deeper. It also embraces the claim based on the performance of a task: for what reason is "recompense" due a man for work done? What is the basis of this obligation? What, in the final analysis, is "the act whereby for each man something becomes his due"?

"It is through creation that the created being first comes to have his rights." [16] By virtue of creation first arises the possibility of saying: "Something is my due." This may sound rather obvious. But on the basis of it Thomas draws this surprising but compelling conclusion: "Therefore, creation itself is not an act of justice; creation is not anyone's due." [17] This means that in the relationship of God to man, there cannot be justice in the strict sense of *reddere suum cuique:* God owes man nothing. "And although God in this way pays each thing its due, yet He Himself is not the debtor." [18] This is surely a new theme. And it is something we shall have to discuss.

At this juncture it must be made clear that no obligation to do justice exists unless it has as its presupposition this idea of the due, the right, the *suum.* That is the meaning of the text: "Now the Just is the object of justice." [19] Now I must confess that it took me a number of years to grasp this point and realize it fully. Only then did I understand, and for the first time, why in the *Summa Theologica* a question, "On Right," issuing from the systematic order that preceded it, came before the treatise on justice.

So if, to the question: "How does man come to have his due," we give the answer: "By reason of creation," we have already said a good deal. Yet we have still not said the last word. The question has still not been given an answer in formal terms.

For stones, plants and animals have also been created, yet we cannot say that they have their due in the strict sense of the word. For "being due" means something like belonging to or being the property of someone.[20] A non-spiritual being, however, cannot properly have anything belonging to it; on the contrary it, itself, belongs to someone else, for instance, to man.

The concept of "being due to," of "right," is such a primordial idea that it cannot be traced back to a prior, subordinating concept. That is to say, it can at best be described, but not defined. We can perhaps say this: Whatever is due to a person, the *suum*, is something that one man may demand of another as owing to him, and him only. And what *is* thus owing can just as well be a thing, perhaps a possession, as an action—and, indeed, not only a private action, such as not being hindered in one's private actions (be it speaking, writing, marrying or going to church), but it can also be an act performed by another, or even the cessation of such an act—anything, for instance, that might be annoying, embarrassing or compromising to a person's good name.

Yet the question persists: on what basis does a man have his due in such a way that it is his inalienable possession? We have nowadays become so accustomed to thinking in the categories of despotism that the great word "inalienable" almost makes us smile. This or that "inalienably" belongs to me! What can such a claim really mean? There is another, more forceful, way of stating the case. That something belongs to a man inalienably means this: the man who does not give a person what belongs to him, withholds it or deprives him of it, is really doing harm to himself; *he* is the one who actually loses something—indeed, in the most extreme case, he even destroys himself. At all events, something incomparably worse befalls him than happens to the one who suffers an injustice: that is how inviolable the right is! That is how strongly the inalienability of the right asserts itself! Socrates has formulated this point over and over again—the person who does an injustice is "to be pitied": [21] "My principle, which has been expressed many times but still bears expressing just once more without any harm, runs like this: my dear Callicles, to receive a box on the ears wrongfully is not the greatest of outrages, nor even to fall into the hands of a murderer or a pick-pocket; . . . to do such injustice to another is a far greater evil for the doer of the injustice than it is for the victim." [22] Expressions such as this should not be construed as simply heroic hyperbole; they are meant as a very precise description of the condition that justice belongs to man's true *being*. All these statements are sober characterizations of a real state of affairs: "The inalienability of right."

What is the basis, then, upon which something comes to be the inalienable due of a person—the presupposition of justice? First of all, the issue might be skirted by giving a less radical answer and saying that a due can arise in many different ways; even Thomas has given such an answer. He says: [23] On the one hand a thing might be due to a man on the basis of agreements, treaties, promises, legal decisions, and so on; on the other hand, it might be due to him on the basis of the nature of the thing, *ex ipsa natura rei* ("and this is called natural right, *ius naturale*"; this is the point where the extremely complicated concept of "natural law" is anticipated). It is true, Thomas adds a remark of the utmost importance to this distinction: it is not exclusive; only on the assumption that the agreement between men, private or public, does not run counter to "the nature of things" may a settlement be the basis for an obligation to a person, that is, of a right. "If, however, a thing of itself is contrary to natural right, the human will cannot make it just." [24]

This is a further help in formulating our question—still the same one—more precisely: something can truly come to be due to me by mere agreement, for instance through a promise; so much so that a person acts against justice and is therefore to be pitied and injures himself, if he withholds it from me. On what, then, does the inalienability, even of this obligation, rest? It is based, we must reply, on the nature of him to whom the obligation is due. There can only be an obligation, in the fullest sense of the term, invulnerable and inalienable, if the bearer of this *suum* is of such a kind that he can claim what is due to him as his right. At this point language only seems to complicate the matter and to have reached the limits of its power to express meaning clearly. This is perfectly natural and we cannot expect anything else. That is what happens when we try to make a primordial, and therefore self-evident concept more intelligible.

Let us take a fictitious example: Suppose I promise my dog something. Let us assume that a sort of customary "right" had been established, that for a certain act the dog should get a reward, with the result that the dog "rightfully" considers it to be something due to him; on my part, let us suppose that I have expressly decided to reward the animal regularly in some definite way. If I were to omit doing so just once, I would, of course, be inattentive, inconstant, forgetful. But in no way would I be unjust in the proper sense. Why not? Because nothing can be inalienably due to a brute; because the presupposition of justice, as well as of injustice—namely, that a "right" in the full sense exists on the side of the other party—does not obtain.[25]

This implies, on the other hand, that we cannot state the basis of a right and, hence, of a judicial obligation, unless we have a concept of man, of human nature.[26] But what if it is claimed that there is, absolutely, no human nature—"*Il n'y a pas de nature humaine*"?[27] This is, in truth, the formal justification for every exercise of totalitarian power—even though such a connection may or may not even enter the heads of those who originate every such existentialist thesis. If, then, there is no human nature on the basis of which alone there is an inalienable obligation to man, how can we escape the consequence: Do what you think fit with man?

Man, however, is a *Person*—a spiritual being, a whole unto himself, a being that exists for itself and of itself, that wills its own proper perfection. Therefore, and for *that very reason*, something *is* due to man in the fullest sense, *for that reason* he does inalienably have a *suum*, a "right" which he can plead against everyone else, a right which imposes upon every one of his partners the obligation at least not to violate it. Indeed, man's personality, "the constitution of his spiritual being by virtue of which he is master of his own actions," even requires (*requirit*), says Thomas,[28] that Divine Providence guide the personality "for his own sake." Moreover, he takes literally that marvellous expression from the *Book of Wisdom:* Even God Himself disposes of us "with great reverence" (*cum magna reverentia*).[29] In the same chapter of the *Summa contra Gentiles* in which this statement occurs the concept of the personality is set forth in all its elements: its freedom, imperishability, and responsibility for the whole of the world. If, on the contrary, man's personality is not acknowledged to be something wholly and entirely real, then right and justice cannot possibly be established.

Nevertheless, even establishing them in this way

still does not get at their deepest roots. For how can human nature be the *ultimate* basis when it is not founded upon itself! At this point we could certainly break off any further delving into the depth. In "moderate" periods, in fact, there would be nothing against it. When the most far-reaching denials of justice take the stage, however, it is no longer enough to go back only to penultimate roots. If man is treated as though simply nothing were due to him as his right, as a *suum*—not merely because the wielding of power has become brutalized, but rather on the basis of a fully articulated theory—at such a time mere reference to the person's freedom and to human rights will obviously not carry us very far. This is simply part of the experiences of our age. Something must be said of the deepest roots of such rights. But more than words are needed. We must learn to experience as reality the knowledge that the establishment of right and justice has not received its fullest and most valid legitimation until we have gone back to the absolute foundation; and that there is no other way to make the demands of justice effective as absolute bounds set the will to power.

This means in concrete terms: Man has inalienable rights because he is created a person by the act of God, that is, an act beyond all human discussion. In the ultimate analysis, then, something is inalienably due to man because he is *creatura*. Moreover, as *crea-*

tura, man has the absolute duty to give another his due. Kant has expressed this in the following manner: "We have a divine Sovereign, and his divine gift to man is man's right." [30] Now a person may very well consider this to be true and may even give it his unqualified consent, but he may nevertheless discover that he himself finds it difficult to draw the conclusion that man's right is unimpeachable because he is created by God. Pious declamation on solemn occasions is not enough. Fundamental truths must constantly be pondered anew lest they lose their fruitfulness. In this lies the significance of meditation: that truth may not cease to be effective in the active life. Perhaps when all the consequences of a false hypothesis suddenly become a direct threat, men in their great terror will become aware that it is no longer possible to call back to true and effective life a truth they have allowed to become remote—just in order to save their bare lives.

It has, I hope, become clear by now that we are not concerned with some vague need for theological trimmings, or with mere edification, but rather with the sober reflective will not to shirk "embarrassing" conclusions and to carry the question through to its ultimate meaning, the question, namely: on what basis is something inalienably due to man, and for what reason does justice first become thinkable and demonstrable as a duty, the violation of which destroys man himself?

But this is not to say that man himself is not possessor and bearer of his right, the *suum*. However true it is that the Creator in His Absoluteness is the *ultimate* foundation for the inalienability of man's rights, still man himself has dues rendered him by all others (indeed he renders dues to all others in turn). "A thing is just not only because it is willed by God, but because it is a debt due to a created being by virtue of the relationship between creature and creature." [31]

This would seem to be the place to speak briefly about one other presupposition of justice. A person may make no formal denial that another should have his due. But he may say that this is no concern of his; that as a man of action it is all the same to him whether in the realm of objective truth one thing goes or another. In other words, as Thomas says, the act of justice not only presupposes that act through which a man comes to have his due; it also presupposes the act of prudence, which means that the truth of real things is transposed into a decision.

It is only in terms of such a situation that it first becomes possible to conceive of one form of injustice that is extremely real, the kind of injustice that rests on man's having lost his contact with truth. To him the question as to whether a man has his due or

not is absolutely and utterly irrelevant. As a result,
something far more radically inhuman than formal
injustice comes to the fore; for human actions are
properly human because they have taken reality as
their measure.[32]

We have made clear that justice can only be discussed meaningfully and fruitfully if it is regarded
in the context of a complete moral doctrine. It is *one*
feature in the sevenfold image of man; the part only
becomes fully intelligible within the whole.

II. DUTY IN RELATION TO "THE OTHER"

"IT IS PROPER to justice, as compared with the other virtues, to direct man in his relations with others; . . . on the other hand the other virtues perfect man only in those matters which befit him in relation to himself." [1] This text from the *Summa Theologica* has the very same meaning as the text-book adage: "*Iustitia est ad alterum*," justice is directed toward the other man. The difference, the separateness of the other party is intended more precisely and literally than may appear at first glance. [2]

What distinguishes justice from love [3] is just this: in the relationship of justice, men confront each other as separate "others," almost as strangers. "Justice properly speaking demands a distinction of supposits, of parties (*diversitatem suppositorum*)." [4] Because father and child are not entirely separate individuals, because the child does much rather belong to the father, and the father feels toward the child almost as he feels toward himself, "so between them there is not a *simpliciter iustum*, the just, simply," [5] not justice in the strict sense. Because the loved one is not

25

properly "someone else," there is no formal justice between those who love. To be just means to recognize the other *as other;* it means to acknowledge there where one cannot love. Justice says: That is another person, who is other than I, and who nevertheless has his own peculiar due. A just man is just, therefore, because he sanctions another person in his very separateness and helps him to receive his due.

It is not superfluous, I think, to spell out every obvious stage of the argument as we have. For nowadays "liquidation" is both concept and reality. Liquidation does not mean punishment, subjugation, conquest, or even execution. Liquidation means extermination merely on the basis of otherness. It would be unrealistic not to see that this ferment: "Whoever is different will be liquidated," works on like a poison, a constant temptation to human thought, destroying or at least menacing it.

That is why it is important to call even the elements of the concept of justice by the right name. Only when we realize what a challenge this concept presents to ordinary current thinking, is it worthwhile meditating it through step by step.

Once we consider the theory of justice as a development of the possibilities of human partnership, of men's relations to "the other," one sign of the erosion and growing aridity of this field in the contemporary human consciousness is the inability of our living tongue to give names to all the various possible violations of partnership enumerated and described in classical Western moral doctrine. We may venture to assert that expressions like "calumny," "malign aspersion," "back-biting," "slander," "tale-bearing" [6] are now in their proper meanings scarcely intelligible to most people—let alone that their essential flavor and expressiveness has long since grown stale and flat. What is "tale-bearing"? Our forebears understood by it: privately spreading evil reports about another, and to that other's friend, no less. And they maintained this was an especially grievous violation of justice, since no man can live without friends.[7] But it is obvious that today we can no longer (rather, never again) describe such an act as "tale-bearing." The fact that current adult speech has not maintained such a usage, that we actually do not have words for such things and many others like them, seems to me most disturbing, and thought-provoking. What term shall we use properly to render *derisio*, the act that violates justice by bringing shame to another through mockery? How designate the special form of justice that goes with it and consists in sparing another man shame?

What I have just said must appear trivial, mere "uplift," utterly unreal, to anyone coming from a world where the concept of "liquidation" is valid. And yet, does it not correspond to the reality of the give-and-take of human life that, varying with the concrete demands of constantly changing situations, one either acknowledges and grants the other his due or else curtails it, deprives him of it, withholds it? The significance of a theory of justice as a virtue lies precisely in considering these manifold ways, giving them names, ordering them, formulating them as ideal images, and making these images familiar to man's consciousness.

Justice, therefore, "consists in living one with another"; [8] the just man has to deal with the other.

In this present inquiry, however, we are only concerned with the just man. Therefore, we are not concerned with "the other," but, rather, with "the one"; not with the one entitled to something, to whom something is due, but with the one bound by duty, the man who has to give to another his due. This is the man who is brought to task by the demands of justice. The one called to justice finds himself by this very fact in the position of a debtor.

Now there are many different degrees and grades of obligation. A person owes the agreed price of an article in a different, stricter way than he is obliged to return thanks for a favor. I am more rigidly bound not to deceive my neighbor than I am obliged to greet him on the street. Thomas has noted this distinction very clearly, between a demand of justice that is legally binding and a demand of justice that is (only) morally binding. I can be compelled to fulfill the first obligation;[9] carrying out the second depends only on my own sense of decency.[10] Moreover, there is a further distinction to be made between demands of justice that are only morally binding: a violation can mean that the person who commits it has done something dishonorable (if he lies, for example); but it may also mean that without being strictly dishonorable, an action has still been "unseemly" (in that it is unkind or unfriendly, for example).

What is common, however, to all these obligations proper to justice is that in every case there is a *debitum*, something owing, a debt. To be just means, then, to owe something and to pay the debt.

One remark: If justice is understood in this way, then, as we have already said, God cannot properly be called "just"—even though, on the other hand, none of the moral virtues, neither fortitude nor temperance, can be ascribed to God with greater justification than justice.[11] God is indebted to no one. "Nothing is owed to the thing created unless it be on the basis of something that preexisted in it . . . and again if this is owing to the thing created, it will again be because of something prior to it. And since we cannot go on to infinity, we must come to something that depends only on the goodness of the divine will" (thus the

Summma Theologica).[12] At most, God's debt is to Himself. "He renders to Himself what is due to Himself." [13] That, however, is not properly a debt and not properly justice. On this point Thomas cites the *Proslogion* of Anselm of Canterbury,[14] in which he expresses the incomprehensibility of the justice of God thus: "When thou dost punish the wicked, it is just; since it agrees with their deserts; and when thou dost spare the wicked, it is also just; since it befits thy Goodness." [15]

Once again: The distinguishing mark of justice is that some debt is to be paid. But am I not doing my duty whenever, in general terms, I fulfill a moral obligation?

It now comes to light that in ethics the fundamental principle of duty, of what one ought to do, of the *debitum*, has its origin in the field of justice. In the Germanic languages, as well as in Latin and Greek, there are words indicating moral obligation that do not at the same time pertain to the realm of justice. "Debt," "debit" and "to be indebted" are obviously related words. And so are "owe" and "ought." The same thing is true of the Latin words *"debere, obligatum esse."* [16] And the Greek word ὀφειλόμενον (which means the same thing as "due, debt, duty") has been related by Plato himself to the meaning: "What has to be paid as a debt to another." [17]

This indicates that the total structure of ethics is revealed, as in a concave mirror, with clearer, sharper outline, in the structure of the act of justice. Something is here revealed that at first glance might otherwise remain hidden. "At first glance (*primo aspectui*)," says Thomas,[18] "it might seem that, as long as a partner does not come forth with a concrete claim, a person may do whatever he thinks fit." But if we consider more deeply, we will find that not only justice but every moral obligation has a personal character, the character of the commitment to the person to whom I am under an obligation. "The notion of duty which is essential to a precept appears in justice." [19]

To do the good, therefore, does not mean that a person obeys some abstract norm, an imperative without imperator. On the contrary, even though it has to do with the most private realm of one's thoughts or the disciplining of appetite, which would seem "at first glance" to belong exclusively to the individual, to do good or evil always means to give or withhold from a person I have to deal with, what is "his." "We are directed to another by all the precepts of the Decalogue," [20]—the Decalogue, which forms a comprehensive *Summa* of the whole field of moral thought.

But who is that "other one" to be, whom man encounters even when he is not being just (or unjust) in the narrow sense? We can answer this question in two ways.

Firstly, the partner can be understood as the community, the "social whole." Obviously I am concerned with the common good not only when I keep or break the civil law, when I pay my taxes or go to the polls; but the common weal is also involved if I am disorderly or indolent in a seemingly private capacity. The common good requires every individual to be good. "The good of any virtue, whether such virtue direct man in relation to himself, or in relation to certain other individual persons, is referable to the common good, to which justice directs so that all acts of virtues can pertain to justice." [21] And, inversely, every sin can in a certain sense be called an "injustice." [22] This is clearly a much broader notion of justice; and for this reason, justice, as a cardinal virtue, cannot be placed on a rank of equality with "fortitude" and "temperance." [23] Thus, Thomas speaks of "legal" or even "general" justice (*iustitia legalis,*[24] *iustitia generalis* [25]) wherein "all virtue is encompassed," which itself is "the most perfect virtue." [26] And Aristotle found words of poetry for it in the *Nichomachean Ethics:* "The evening star nor the morning star is as glorious" as justice.[27]

Secondly, to say "every moral act has the structure of justice" can also mean that whoever does good or evil stands in relation to God as His "partner," to Whom he is giving or withholding His due. "It belongs to general justice (*iustitia generalis*) to do good

in relation to the community or in relation to God." [28]
So while a man obeys or breaks commandments, he is
not dealing with "objective legality" but, rather, with
a personal lawgiver, with "some other person."

Nevertheless, the obligation that is to be fulfilled
within the scope of justice is utterly distinct from the
obligation the man of fortitude or the man of temperance is under—not only in substance but also in
structure; not only in the *What* but also in the *How*.
The distinction is this: We are able to judge from external appearances what is "objectively" just or unjust,
but it does not make any sense to ask what is "objectively" brave and cowardly, temperate and in-
temperate.

Justice is realized above all in an external act; "in
the realm of what is just or unjust, what man does
externally is the main point at issue." [29] On the other
hand, in the field of fortitude and temperance man's
inner state has primarily to be considered and only
then, secondarily, his external act. I cannot simply
consider a person's act, and on that basis decide
whether he is brave, cowardly, temperate or dissolute;
I would have to know more of the person, I would
have to know what his disposition is. The justice of an
act, on the other hand, can be judged even from the
outside, by an impartial third party. How much wine
should I drink without violating the virtue of tem-

perance? No stranger could determine that. But, how much do I owe the inn-keeper? That can be "objectively" verified by anyone.

This peculiarity of justice, however, that it should first and foremost be realized in an external act—(arising, as it does, from my discharging my obligations—whether I do so readily or not, whether I am in need or not, whether my creditor is rich or poor; Kant says: "The other person may be in need or not, he may be in distress or not; but if it is a question of his right, then I am obliged to satisfy it" [30])—this distinguishing mark of justice bears the closest possible relation to the fact that it has, essentially, to do with the "other person." "The other person" is not affected by my subjective disposition, by what I intend, think, feel, or will, but only by what I do. Only by an external act will the other receive what is *his*, his due. "Men are ordained to one another by outward acts, *per exteriores actus*, whereby men live in communion with one another." That is a sentence from the *Summa Theologica*.[31] It is also the reason why, so Thomas says, in the realm of justice good and evil are judged purely on the basis of the deed itself, regardless of the inner disposition of the doer; the point is not how the deed accords with the doer, but rather, how it affects "the other person." [32]

The reverse of this statement is also valid. Not only

34

is the act of justice an external act, but every external act belongs to the field of justice. Whatever external act a person performs, it is either just or unjust.

Of course, this does *not* imply that there are no external acts of fortitude, temperance, wantonness as well. Nevertheless, Thomas does maintain the proposition: *"Circa actiones est iustitia";* [33] in any outward act, justice or injustice come into play. He gives an example: "When through anger one man strikes another, justice is destroyed in the undue blow; while gentleness (*mansuetudo*) is destroyed in the immoderate anger." [34] Such a case of coming to blows and of injured "gentleness" may not seem particularly relevant, but the thesis naturally extends much farther. It also implies, for example, that the whole field of sexual aberration, not adultery and rape only, contains an element of injustice. We are not used to perceiving or considering this point. We are apt to concentrate almost exclusively on the subjective significance of dissoluteness as it affects the one who performs the act; whereas it usually escapes us that it is the order of our communal life, and the realization of the common good, which are equally affected, and the more dangerously so the more "external" is the act in question. [35]

Thomas de Vio, also called Cajetan, the commentator of the *Summa Theologica,* formulates a possible

objection to this idea in his commentary.[36] He says
that an act can be considered from three different
points of view, and the *Summa Theologica* names all
three of them: the act can be treated in its relationship and fittingness (*commensuratio*) to the one performing it; in its relationship and fittingness to the
other person; and thirdly, it can be regarded in itself.
Now this is the objection: Does not Thomas fuse the
second and third consideration of an act and confuse
the one with the other? Cajetan replies, interpreting
Thomas: *Hoc non te moveat*, "don't let this trouble
you"; if "act" means the same as "external act," then
it is related to the other person *of itself*, by the very
fact that it is an external act. Consequently, it amounts
to the same to say "the act regarded in itself" and "the
act regarded in its relation to the other person."

To sum up: *Every* external act is of social consequence. We do not speak without being heard; we do
not make use of a thing without using our own or
another's property. It is justice, however, that distinguishes what is one's own from that which belongs
to another.[37] Whoever teaches is not merely concerned
with true and false, above all not with a "private"
view of what is true, nor with "personal" opinions.
He is quite as concerned with the just or unjust. To
teach untruth is not only wrong, but unjust as well.
All ten commandments are *praecepta justitiae*.[38] The
whole field of the *vita activa*, also called the *vita civilis*

36

by Thomas—"all of which is defined with reference to our relations with other people" [39]—is the field of justice.

If it is possible to designate the "just thing" apart from the inner condition of the one who performs it, is it perhaps possible, too, to think that a person can *do* the "just thing" without *being* just? In the realm of justice there is actually something approaching a separation of deed and intention. In his treatise on law Thomas says: "The mode of doing acts of justice, which falls under the precept, is that they be done in accordance with right; but not that they be done from the habit of justice" [40]—a formula that is very sober and realistic, it is true, but pretty pointed as well. It states that there is no need for a man to *be* just in order that he may *do* "the just thing." Whence it also follows that a person can *do* something unjust without *being* unjust. And this is possible because there is something "objectively" unjust, whereas it is meaningless to speak of something "objectively" cowardly or patient.

Thus, if a soldier withdraws from a dangerous assignment because he has misunderstood an order,[41] he does not thereby commit an act of cowardice. However, if anyone takes as his own something belonging to another—because he too has misunderstood—he is performing an unjust act, because something is taken from that other person which, in fact, belongs to him.

Yet he is not therefore unjust. Once again, this would be quite inconceivable with reference to the other virtues. Whoever behaves himself in an unruly manner, whoever does "something unruly," *is* unruly—at least at that moment. But whoever, carried away by some passion, injures another, commits an unrighteous act, does something unjust, it is true. Nonetheless, he is not necessarily unjust for this reason.[42]

A side comment: Should not all this be of some significance for the political realm of discourse, which is of course concerned with what is just and unjust? Does it not imply, for example, that it may be quite possible and logical to reject a certain political objective as "objectively unjust"—and even to combat it with intensity—*without* at the same time bringing the moral integrity of one's opponent into the discussion?

Our present theme, however, is justice as a *virtue*. Now it undoubtedly does pertain to a man's righteousness not only to do "the just thing" but also *to be* just as well. Thomas quotes the *Nichomachean Ethics:* [43] It is an easy matter to do what the just man does; it is difficult, however, for one who does not possess justice to do the just thing *in the way* the just man does it. And he adds: "That is, with promptitude and pleasure." [44] Wherever justice in the full sense is done, the external act is an expression of an inner assent: the other is acknowledged and confirmed in what is due to him. But what *is* due to him cannot be decided from the subjective, inner disposition of the one bound by the obligation, however intent on justice it may be. Intention is not enough for the realization of justice. What is due to a person, what is an obligation, can and must be ascertained *objectively*.

"The mean of justice consists in a certain proportion of equality between the external thing and the external person (*ad personam exteriorem*)." [45]

III. THE RANK OF JUSTICE

WHEN THE QUESTION of the rank of a virtue—its place in the scale of eminence among the virtues—is raised in traditional moral teaching, this is not just a whimsical game played with allegorical figures of speech. It is, rather, a very precise delineation of the image of the good man. The question signifies: What makes man fundamentally good and righteous? Understood in this way, the question as to the supreme virtue is usually answered in accordance with the virtue most highly esteemed at a particular period, such as "decency," or "self-control," or "imperturbability," or "courage."

Now Thomas says that man reveals his true being in its greatest purity when he is just; justice is the highest of the three moral (in the strict sense) virtues: justice, fortitude, and temperance. The good man is above all the just man. On this point Cicero[1] is cited in the *Summa Theologica:* "Good men are so called chiefly from their justice," "the luster of virtue appears above all in justice." [2] Like the outer porch to the temple, this pre-Christian wisdom is in harmony with

Christian doctrine, for Holy Scripture speaks more than eight hundred times of "justice" and "the just man," by which it means no less than "the good, the holy man."

It seems that this insight into the rank of justice is gradually becoming more generally recognized in our time. First, the image of the good man had been modelled after a rather bourgeois concept of "morality," and, later, after an isolated ideal of "the heroic"; and we have learned that injustice corrupts the fruits of fortitude and that "fortitude without justice is a source (*iniquitatis materia*) of evil." [3] So it is once more possible for us to see that justice, of all the human, natural virtues, is literally the fundamental virtue.

This rank of justice can be established in many ways.

Firstly: Thomas says justice claims a higher rank because it not only orders man in himself but also the life of men together. Justice reaches out beyond the individual subject, because in a certain sense it is itself the *bonum alterius*, the "good of another." The as it were concrete efficacy of Good is revealed in a higher manner in justice. For it is in the nature of Good to be "*diffusivum sui*," not to be limited to its place of origin but to pour itself out, to work outside itself, to be shared with others, to shine forth. "A thing is more eminently good the more fully and widely it radiates its goodness." [4] For as that man is most utterly evil who allows his wickedness to hold sway not only over himself but over his friends as well; so is that man most utterly good who not only uses his goodness for himself but for others, too.[5] Now this applies to justice in a higher degree than to the virtues of fortitude and temperance.

Secondly: not only do the object and material of justice (*objectum sine materia*)[6] establish its higher rank, but the *subject* does so, too. Exactly how is the subject of justice to be distinguished from the subject of the other virtues? Is not the subject always man himself, the human person? It is not easy to arrive at an interpretation which makes it clear why St. Thomas is so emphatic on this point.

The human person is naturally the subject of all moral attitudes and decisions. Yet this subject is not a simple, homogeneous reality; above all else it is an entity composed of body and soul. Various virtues can only be thought of because man is a *corporeal* being. A pure spirit cannot be chaste (in the sense of *temperantia*); and such a being has just as little need to moderate the stirring of anger or even to suppress fear. Man, on the other hand, who strives mightily to realize courage and temperance, is beset with the claims of the body; he is the subject of fortitude and temperance insofar as he has bodily existence. But this does not hold true of justice. The demands of justice beset man at his spiritual core. Man is the subject of justice to the extent that he is a spiritual being. Now inasmuch as the power immediately supporting the act of justice is a spiritual desire; "inasmuch as justice," Thomas says, "is in the more excellent part of the soul"; [7] inasmuch as the demand on man that he be just is directed at the innermost kernel of his spiritual will, justice holds the foremost rank above all the other moral virtues.

The case is conceivable in which a man has so succeeded, by unceasing *askesis*, in his efforts to create order within himself, that his senses no longer disturb the working of his spiritual soul. What is left for him to do? Well, now, at last, he could achieve what up till now he was prevented from doing, something that he could never realize in its essence: Good itself, properly human Good. But what is that? Simply this: that man attains to his true treasure and proper realization of himself when he sees the Truth and "does the Truth." "The good of man, insofar as he is man, consists in his reason's being perfected in the knowledge of truth and his subordinated appetitive powers' being ruled according to the directions of reason." [8] Behind this statement of St. Thomas' stands the thought that in the vision of truth, in contemplation, man attains his proper fulfillment and also the full realization of "human Good." But just where does moral virtue find its place within this scheme? Above all, what is the

43

connection between justice and "man's good," which is "the good of reason" or, simply, Truth? This is the answer Thomas gives: the good of reason shines more brightly in justice than in any of the other moral virtues; justice is closer to reason.[9] Indeed, the good of reason consists in justice as its proper effect (*sicut in proprio effectu*).[10]

In his treatise on the virtue of fortitude St. Thomas raises the question as to whether or not fortitude is the highest of the cardinal virtues. Once more the reply sets out from the notion of "Man's good" (*bonum hominis*); and then, working from this idea, which implies "the Good of reason," Truth, he formulates the order of the virtues: "Prudence has the good essentially. Justice effects this good; whereas the other virtues. . . ."[11] But here it is impossible to suppress the following objection: Is not an act of fortitude or restraint of desire a "realization of the Good," too? This objection, however, needs to be clarified. The meaning of the term "act of fortitude" is rather complex. The bravery of an act—for example, if someone risks his life for the community—is a purely internal process, the mastery of fear and of the natural impulse to live. But, on the other hand, the external act of risking one's life, insofar as this is an obligation to the community, is an act of justice. More exactly then, the objection is this: Is not the restraining of fear and desire, as in courage and temperance, likewise "doing

Good"? On that score Thomas in fact gives the answer: No! In considering the cardinal virtues, it is only through prudence and justice that man is simply and directly (*simpliciter*) directed toward the good.[12] And for that reason he awards them precedence. But what of fortitude and temperance? The statement our objection interrupted goes on to give the answer: "Whereas the other virtues safeguard this good, inasmuch as they moderate the passions lest they do lead man away from reason's good."[13] But how is this to be understood? To exercise restraint and moderation, to overcome fear of death, is not yet "doing Good." These are not properly realizations of human Good. What are they, then? They create the basis—indeed the indispensable basis—for the proper realization of Good.

Thorough confirmation and corroboration of this surprising statement comes from the experience of the great ascetics. Their experience indicates that the real testing of, as well as the most serious threat to, the inner man, begins only after that basis has been established.

Once more: "Now to be a thing essentially ranks before effecting it, and the latter ranks before safeguarding it by removing obstacles thereto; wherefore amongst the cardinal virtues prudence ranks first, justice second; fortitude third, temperance fourth."[14]

We now see clearly why Thomas can say that justice not only has its seat in the will, i.e., in the power that is formally directed towards the realization of Good, but also that through justice the will is applied to its proper act.[15] *Iustitia est humanum bonum*, "Justice is the human good." [16] This conception of the rank which justice occupies can be assessed as a permanent element in the traditional wisdom of the West, quite apart from Thomas. We find a formulation of this very view in the most extreme Platonic wing of that tradition, in Plotinus: Justice simply means "doing one's own work" and "fulfilling one's own task." [17]

The rank of justice is also asserted negatively. "Among all the moral virtues it is justice wherein the use of right reason appears chiefly . . . hence the undue (*indebitus*) use of reason appears chiefly in the vices opposed to justice." [18] The worst disruption of order in the field of things naturally human, i.e., the true perversion of "human Good," bears the name injustice.

It is therefore of considerable importance that man prepare himself to encounter historical realizations of evil in which a high degree of "morality" is joined with a considerable measure of "heroism," but which nonetheless remain thoroughly and unsurpassingly inhuman and evil, because at the same time they embody uttermost injustice. We would do well to bear in mind that the uttermost perversion of mankind lies not in excess, which can be easily read in man's bearing and behavior, but in injustice, which, being essentially of the spirit, is not so readily distinguishable. We ought to be prepared to find that the most powerful embodiment of evil in human history, the Antichrist, might well appear in the guise of a great ascetic. This is, in fact, the almost unanimous lesson of historical thinking in the West.[19] Whoever does not understand that it is injustice which is natural man's worst destroyer, and the reason why, will be thrown into overwhelming confusion by the experiences announced in such visions. Above all, he will be powerless to recognize the historical heralds of the abyss. For, even while he watches out in the wrong direction, the forces of destruction will establish their mastery right before his very eyes.

IV. THE BASIC FORMS OF JUSTICE

WHEN MAY JUSTICE be said to prevail in a nation? For
the place of justice is in communal life; in an inquiry
concerning the realization of justice, we have to direct our attention to the life of the community—to the
family, the industrial organization, to the nation organized as a state. One might almost say that the subject of justice is the "community," although of course
it is only the person, and, therefore, the individual,
who can be just in the strict sense of the word. But to
repeat our question: When may justice be said to prevail in a community?

Plutarch, Diogenes Laertius, Stobaeus have given
answers in the form of maxims ascribed to the "Seven
Sages." Their replies demonstrate that our question
has always been a subject of philosophic speculation.
The almost incredible timeliness of their answers
proves how very little the passing of time affects this
particular field. Thales (of whom Diogenes Laertius
reports several very pointed maxims) gives this reply
to the question about the strangest thing he had seen
in his life: "A tyrant who has grown old." [1] The

48

statesman Thales says: "If there is neither excessive wealth nor immoderate poverty in a nation, then justice may be said to prevail." [2] Bias—(to whom is ascribed a thoughtful saying, also quoted by Thomas,[3] of but three words: ἀρχὴ ἄνδρα δείξει, mastery reveals the man [4])—gives this answer: "When everyone in the state fears the laws as he would fear a tyrant." [5] Solon replies with a well-aimed remark: "Justice rules whenever a criminal is accused and judged in the same way by all those he has *not* injured as he would be by the person to whom he has done some injury." [6] This means that the true character of a criminal wrong is not so much the loss of some possession, the injury to health or life, but, rather, the implicit threat to the entire order of community life, affecting every member. Once this is recognized by everyone, justice can be said to prevail in that state. A series of noteworthy maxims of the Spartan Cheilon have also been handed down to us by Diogenes Laertius. Here is just one example: Three things are surpassingly difficult: Keeping a secret, accepting an injustice, making good use of one's leisure.[7] To the question about the just state, Cheilon answers that it is realized whenever the citizen habitually pays most attention to the laws and least to the orators.[8] Pittakos, himself a ruler in his own city, Mytilene, touches in his answer upon the form of government. He says that if it is not possible for the wicked to rule in a *polis*, and if it is likewise not possible for the good to be excluded from ruling, then justice is a reality.[9]

Anyone can see that these replies are not so much a matter of stating formal definitions but, rather, of giving some characterizations that have been arrived at empirically, i.e., of the precipitate of experience.

St. Thomas' answer might have run like this: Justice rules in a community or state whenever the three basic relations, the three fundamental structures of communal life, are disposed in their proper order: firstly, the relations of individuals to one another (*ordo partium ad partes*); secondly, the relations of the social whole to the individuals (*ordo totius ad partes*); thirdly, the relations of the individuals to the social whole (*ordo partium ad totum*). These three basic relationships correspond to the three basic forms of justice: reciprocal, or mutually exchanged justice (*iustitia commutativa*), which orders the relation of individual to individual partner; ministering justice (*iustitia distributiva*), which brings order to the relations between the community as such and the individuals who are its members; legal or general justice (*iustitia legalis, iustitia generalis*), which orders the members' relations to the social whole.

The hallmark of all three fundamental forms of justice is some kind of *indebtedness*, different in character in each case. The obligation to pay the tax collector is different in kind from that of settling my book dealer's account. And the legal protection the state owes the individual is due to me, in principle, in quite a different fashion than my neighbor owes me the return of a loan.

Moreover, a different *subject* is involved in each of these three fundamental forms. To say that commutative justice orders the relations between one individual and another is quite obviously an inadequate formulation. Evidently it is not justice that orders. It is the just man, it is *man* who orders. In the last analysis it is man, and hence the individual person, who supports and realizes all three fundamental forms of justice. Yet the individual is implicated in three different ways. The individual as associate of other individuals sustains commutative justice, whereas the subject of legal justice is, to be sure, once again the individual, but now as the associate of the species, as it were, as a member of the community, as a "subject." So, too, the "social whole" cannot in any concrete sense make distributive justice a reality; again it is rather the individual man—if not the king, then the dictator, the chief of state, the civil servant or even, in a consistent democracy, the individual, insofar as he has a determining role in administering the common good.

One is tempted to give a diagram of these structures, though such a sketch has to be not only inexact, but in many details plainly inadequate. Yet inasmuch as that inescapable inadequacy brings into clear focus the necessity for corrections in what has already been said, it will not be wasted effort to give some consideration to a diagram.* And in trying to determine that inadequacy the reader will find that he is personally participating in the present discussion. He will find himself drawn into a controversial discussion and compelled to give a clear-cut interpretation of social reality, which means human reality. In what respect, then, is the schema wrong?

Thomas would see the inaccuracy above all in that the individual and the social whole are represented as separate, sharply distinguished realities, whereas in actual fact the individual who "confronts" the social whole is at the same time included in it as a member. Thomas would always insist that in actual fact individual persons, *personae privatae*,[10] have a reality, an ontological status of their own, and cannot be simply reduced to the reality of the social whole. The human community, the state, Thomas says, is so constructed that the deeds and works of the individual are not of necessity the deeds and works of the whole; and similarly a functioning of the whole as such is possible that is not identical with the functioning of the individual member.[11]

It may be objected that these are abstract specula-

* Confer the diagram on p. 121.

52

tions. But in order to arrive, for instance, at a sound judgment on the question of collective guilt, we have to go back to this ultimate foundation.

A consistent individualism would raise a totally different objection to our diagram—because its premise is a different interpretation of basic human relations. The individualist's criticism would be that there are in reality only individuals, and that, when an individual confronts the social totality, *one* individual confronts *many* individuals. For him the social whole is not a reality of a special order. Therefore he admits of only one single type of justice—commutative justice—because individuals always have to do with other individuals. Every phase of man's communal life, in the family as well as in the state, is a compromise between the interests of individuals with equal rights.

A third—the collectivist—interpretation is more immediately timely. It predicates that there is no such thing as an individual capable of entering into relationships in his own right. Above all, no *private* relations between individuals exist. Man's life has a totally public character because the individual is adequately defined only through his membership in the social whole which is the only reality. Of course no social theory can alter the fact that individuals are actually in relation with each other. Even in the most totalitarian state, I address actual men and hence individuals whenever

I speak. However, all such relations can at any moment be interpreted as "official," if they have not been official in the first place. Suddenly I find myself no longer associating with "my" friend, "my" wife, "my" father, but with a co-functionary in the state cause, i.e., with a state functionary. As a result, all human relationships are simultaneously subordinated to the yardstick of fulfilling a function, and may abruptly cease to exist when I do not conform to the stipulated norm. Appalling examples of this type are part and parcel of contemporary experience. Needless to say that from this point of view the concept of commutative justice becomes meaningless; [12] as, equally, the concept of distributive justice, which proclaims that an individual has rights not only in his relations with other individuals but with the social whole as well. And even the seemingly unaffected concept of *iustitia legalis*, which formulates the individual's obligation toward the functions of the state, has in the last analysis become unthinkable. The notion of justice has ceased to be applicable in any sense whatsoever.

The end result of this reasoning seems decidedly noteworthy. It becomes evident that the very essence of justice is threatened the moment the serious claim were made that these three fundamental structures of the communal life (structures that are independent of each other), and hence the three basic forms of justice, simply do not exist. It seems that at least such a threefold structure is required to do justice to the extremely complex reality contained in the all-too-glibly treated twin concepts "Individual and Society." But of course the decisive factor is not the purely intellectual admission of conceptual distinctions. The important thing, rather, is that justice prevail and become a reality, in its threefold form.

V. RECOMPENSE AND RESTITUTION

COMPENSATORY or commutative justice is, as it were, the classic form of justice, for several reasons. First of all, in the relations between individuals, every partner actually confronts an "other person" quite independent of himself; the *"ad alterum"* is a fully realized fact. In the other two fundamental relations, however, the individual does not properly "confront" the "we" (those with whom he is in contact and who are associated with him) as another separate person. Then, too, the partner's equal rights are unreservedly realized only in the situation of commutative justice. But here a second element in the true concept of justice is suggested: "Justice is simply (*simpliciter*) between those who are simply equal, but where there is no absolute equality between them, neither is there absolute justice." [1]

One consequence of this is that this kind of justice is not thinkable in the relations between God and man. "Commutative justice, strictly so-called, cannot be said of God because it would presuppose an equality between God, Who gives, and the creature, who receives." [2] Just in the manner of commutative justice is the individual who gives the other person, the un-related individual, the stranger, what is his due—neither less nor more. To be sure, *commutatio* (changing hands, the transfer of a thing from one person to another [3]) also applies in the giving of a gift. Yet to make a present is not an act of justice because the thing given is in no sense owed, not a *debitum*.[4] On this score, Thomas insists most ener-getically that justice should not go beyond what is owed. This is not, I think, mere pedantry. Still less is it a matter of niggardly minimalism. Rather it means, soberly and without romantic illusion: the ideal image of *iustitia commutativa* demands that a man be able to acknowledge the rights particularly of the stranger, whether he be in fact unrelated, or felt to be alien, perhaps because he suddenly appears as "competitor," threatening one's own interests, a person whose affairs are "none of my business," whom I "don't care for," to whom I would not dream of giving a gift; against whom, rather, I have to hold my ground and assert myself. To this very stranger I have to give his due, neither more nor less: this is justice.

The charge of minimalistic niggardliness could also be raised against contractual agreements, the estab-lished form of balancing interests, which is why *iustitia commutativa* has also been called "contract justice." There are persons and movements who, in an unrealistic over-valuation of "community" ideals regard the balancing of interests by contract as an inferior form of regulating human relationships, since they are based only on the "cold" calculation of one's own advantage.[5]

It is true that the partners to a contract are "interested parties." The very meaning of a contract is, indeed, to mark the limits of each party's rights and to guarantee one party's claim to a certain return as much as the other's obligation to make that return. If love says: "Whatever belongs to me should belong to the one I love, too," justice proclaims: "To each his own." Which means that what is yours is yours, and what is mine is mine. In relations built on love, that is, in relations truly "shared" between man and man, there is no call for either contract, or, in the strict sense, for justice.

Countering the romantic over-valuation of a special form of communal life, we have to bear in mind that, if the contract represents a balancing of interests, it also represents a form of mutual understanding. We perceive only one part of the reality if we consider nothing but the self-assertion of the party to a contract. The other part, at least where a just and equitable contract is concerned (which is here taken for granted—though a just contract is not a declaration of love, but remains a method of balancing interests) is the mutual acknowledgment of the parties. A contract implies a genuine obligation and tie, as well as an expressly affirmed restriction of one's own interest by the other party's interest. The reality of a contractual balance of interests includes the faithful fulfillment of the contract. It involves the acknowledgment of the principle of equality between service and counter-service. To sum up: a contract is an instrument not of self-assertion only, but also of rendering the "other" his due.

However true it may be that man's communal life cannot attain its fullest realization through *iustitia commutativa* alone, it is no less true that in its ideal image the irreducible core of social relations finds expression, that it is the foundation which even the higher and richer forms of mutual agreement require.

It is not easy to exhaust the implications of the proposition in the *Summa Theologica* which says: The act of justice which orders the association of individuals with one another [6] is *restitutio*, recompense, restoration. A French translation tends to weaken what Thomas has said and makes an interpretative insertion to the effect that it is not a question of *the* act of commutative justice but of its principal act (*acte première*).[7] However, the sense of even this interpretation is that in the field of *iustitia commutativa* "restitution" occupies a unique place. As a matter of fact there is nothing about any other act in Thomas.

What, then, is *restitutio?* Thomas himself gives the

answer. "It is seemingly the same as once more (*iterato*) to re-instate a person in the possession or dominion of his thing." [8] It is, then, a *re*storation, a *re*compense, a *re*turning. What are we to make of these reiterations? I think we would lose insight into the meaning hidden here if we were to reduce *restitutio* simply to its present significance of restitution, that is, of returning another person's property and making reparation for some illegally wrought injury. [9] Rather, we are here concerned with "surprise" formulations that point to some unexpressed thought which is self-evident to Thomas but not to us. A key to what is meant here can be found in such familiar phrases as: "To give to each his own." There is something very much to the point in Schopenhauer's objection: "If it is his own, there is no need to *give* it to him." [10] A condition of justice is the startling fact that a man may *not* have what is nonetheless "his own"—as the very concept of "something due a person" implies. Consequently, the recognition of the *suum* can rightly be called re-storation, re-stitution, re-compense, re-instatement to an original right. And this does not apply only to cases like theft, fraud and robbery (Thomas speaks of *commutationes involuntariae*, changes in original ownership which take place against the will of one of the partners [11]). It is not only in this area that it is meaningful to speak of *restitutio;* but wherever one man owes another something—(even in such voluntary obligations as buying, renting, or borrowing [12])—or wherever due respect is shown and due thanks are expressed, to give what is due is always "restitution."

The state of equilibrium that properly corresponds to man's essence, to his original, "paradisiac" state, is constantly thrown out of balance, and has constantly to be "restored" through an act of justice. Nor must the disturbance be necessarily understood as injustice, though the fact that the act of justice is called *restitutio* presupposes that injustice is the prevalent condition in a world dominated by opposing interests, the struggle for power, and hunger. To bring solace and order into the conflict of contending interests which by their nature are legitimate opposites and not easily reconcilable, to impose on them, as it were, a posterior order, is the office and task of commutative justice. The establishment of equity has as its premise that there is no natural equality, or that it exists not yet, or no longer. Just above all is the man who does not become inured and hardened to disorder, not even to a disorder he may have originated himself at first impulse (to become a man means learning to be unjust, says Goethe). The just man recognizes when wrong has been done, admits his own injustice and endeavors to eradicate it. Who would deny that we touch here the sore spot in all reciprocal relationships, and that the basic way to realize commutative justice does in fact have the character of restitution?

Yet, as has already been said, we need not turn our attention only to compensation for injustice. Man's every act "disturbs" the stable equilibrium, since every act turns the doer into either a debtor or a creditor. And since men are constantly becoming indebted to one another, the demand is constantly raised to pay that debt by an act of "restitution." Therefore, the equality that characterizes justice cannot be finally and definitely established at any one time, it cannot be arrested. It must, rather, be constantly re-established, "restored anew" (*iterato*). It has to be "re-instated." The "return to equilibrium" which, Thomas says, occurs in *restitutio*,[13] is an unending task. This means that the dynamic character of man's communal life finds its image within the very structure of every act of justice. If the basic act of commutative justice is called "*re*-stitution," the very word implies that it is never possible for men to realize an ideal and definitive condition. What it means is, rather, that the fundamental condition of man and his world is provisory, temporary, non-definitive, tentative, as is proved by the "patchwork" character of all historical activity, and that, consequently, any claim to erect a definitive and unalterable order in the world must of necessity lead to something inhuman.

VI. THE JUSTICE OF GOVERNMENT

WHOEVER speaks of distributive justice has to speak of government. That is why a discussion of *iustitia distributiva* is the very center of the theory of justice.

Let us recall the characteristic structure of distributive justice by reminding ourselves that an individual man is not confronted with another individual only, nor even with many individuals. He is confronted by the social whole. It becomes clear at once that the two partners are not of equal rank, not only because many are more than one, but also because the common weal belongs to another and higher order than the good of the individual.[1] Nevertheless, it is the individual who is the partner with the claim in this relationship. He is the one to whom something is due. This means that, on the other hand, the social whole is the partner bound by an obligation. The social whole ranks higher than the individual, and yet it is bound by an obligation. We have already said that this concept cannot be realized by a consistent individualism, and certainly not by collectivism.

Hence the claim expressed in the ideal image of

iustitia distributiva is formally directed toward the social whole, the governor, the ruler, the law-giver. Man, as administrator of the common weal, is brought to account and is obliged to give the individual members of the whole their due. The ideal image of distributive justice, however, does not authorize individuals to determine and assert on their own initiative what is due to them on the part of the social whole. But though they are not so authorized, this does not mean that such a premise would be impossible and intrinsically counter to justice. Rather: where justice is under discussion, whenever it is said, "Thou shalt be just," the reference is not to the claimant, but to the one who has to grant the due. In the case of *iustitia distributiva* this means: the claim and appeal is directed to man insofar as he represents the social whole. The fact that at first thought we no longer consider the administrator of the common weal as a person, that we have ceased to visualize him as an individual open to personal approach and consider him rather as a faceless mechanism, shows the dangerous extent to which we are already conditioned by collectivist thinking.

One more point has to be considered in order to make clear the structure of distributive justice. There is an obligation due to the individual in his relation towards the social whole that is in principle different from his due as creditor towards debtor in a situation of commutative justice. What belongs to him and the way it belongs to him are quite different. In the case of commutative justice, a creditor has the right to receive the equivalent of a service he has rendered or reparation for a loss he has sustained. It is his due as something belonging to him exclusively as an individual. But what is the individual's due in the case of *iustitia distributiva?* Nothing belongs to him as exclusively his, *non id quod est proprium;* all that belongs to him is a share in something common to everyone, *id quod est commune.*[2] In this instance the individual is not an independent, separate party to a contract with claims equal to those of his partner, as in *iustitia commutativa.* He is faced with a partner of higher rank, of which he himself is a part. "Distributive justice . . . distributes common goods proportionately."[3] "There are two kinds of justice: the one consists in mutual giving and receiving . . . the other consists in distribution, *in distribuendo,* and is called distributive justice; whereby a ruler or steward gives to each what his rank deserves."[4]

Several tangible consequences follow from this.

Firstly: In the situation of commutative justice, the due can be as surely calculated and determined by the party entitled to it as by the party obligated to pay it—or even by an impartial third party. That is *not* possible in the case of *iustitia distributiva*. Determining what is the due of any one person can only be effected from the position and viewpoint of the one responsible for the common weal, for the very reason that a due and fitting share in the common good is involved. In both cases an obligation is established. But in the one case, the obligation is paid, in the other case it is allotted. If I sell my house, I can leave the price due to me to be ascertained by a third party, or I can bargain with the buyer, or I can simply demand it. If, however, following the practice of equitable sharing of burdens, some compensation is due me from the state to cover damage to my house during wartime, I cannot determine independently what is rightfully mine. Only the responsible guardian of the common weal can establish what is due to me, as he is concerned with the *bonum commune*. Secondly: In the case of *iustitia distributiva* justice and equity cannot be achieved by consideration of the actual value only. In commutative justice such an approach is both possible and meaningful. A just price can be determined without reference to the person of the buyer or seller, simply by taking into consideration the market value of the object that is to be sold. In this case justice and equity consist in the *aequalitas rei ad rem*, as Thomas formulates it.[5] In the relation between the social whole and individuals, on the contrary, what is just is determined as "whatever corresponds to the thing's proportion to the person." [6] That means that the one who administers the common good may not consider the object of the obligation alone. Rather, he has to keep the subjects of the obligation in view as well. He must consider the individuals with whom he has to deal. Thus, in the case of indemnity for war damage, the true value of the damage is not the only thing to be considered. Justice might demand the taking into account of such factors as whether or not the damage has completely impoverished the person, whether or not he had already made any other great sacrifice for the social whole (i.e., in the case of a refugee or a battle casualty). Thus, the compromise that has to be effected [7] both in distributive justice and in commutative justice has a quite distinct character in each instance. In the first case it is a "proportional" equality (*aequalitas proportionis*), in the other a purely numerical, "quantitative" equality (*aequalitas quantitatis*). In the same place in his commentary on the *Nichomachean Ethics*,[8] following again Aristotle,[9] Thomas has pointed out that this distinction is the same as the difference between a geometric and an arithmetic proportion.

The reader may possibly get the impression that what has been said of distributive justice up to this point has a distinctly "totalitarian" tinge. It is part and parcel of the intellectual and political atmosphere of the day that this should be an almost compulsive reaction. The idea that there is in distributive justice a single authority that administers the common good and that is able, by virtue of its own rights, to decide what and how much is due to me, is almost inevitably linked with that other idea of enslaving the individual and encroaching upon his rights. And at the same time a picture of "Democracy" looms up alongside it as the (supposedly) only remaining alternative, that leaves no room for genuine authority and thus again veers toward despotism or has it close in its wake. In view of this literally fatal choice, it is decisive that we should recognize the ideal image of *iustitia distributiva* and make it a reality. Two things are combined in this image: the affirmation of genuine authority and at the same time the recognition of the individual person to whom his right is absolutely due from the social whole.

It is this very absoluteness, however, which gives rise to the emotional objection. Rationally formulated, it would amount to something like this: You say that in the individual's relationship with the social whole something is due to the individual, but not, as in the case of commutative justice, as an exclusive personal right; rather, it is his share in a property common to all. But are there not things to which I have an irrevocable, a truly absolute claim, even when confronted with the social whole, with the state?

68

The state, we may note, occupies a unique place in the scale that extends from the individual to the whole of mankind; more than anything else, it represents the "social whole." The idea of the common good is its distinctive attribute. A nation (in the midst of other nations) ordered in a state is the proper, historically concrete image of man's communal life. *Communitas politica est communitas principalissima*, "political community is community in the highest degree." [10] In the fullest sense the state alone incorporates, realizes and administers the *bonum commune*. That does not mean, however, that the family, the community, free associations, and the Church are not important for the realization of the common good, too. But it means that the harmonizing and integration of nearly all men's functions occurs only in the political community. In the state alone is sovereignty vested and with it the authority and the power to maintain the *bonum commune* in its fullest sense—an authority which includes the full right to impose punishment. "Since the state is a perfect society, the ruler of the state possesses full power of compulsion. Therefore, he can inflict irreparable punishment such as death or mutilation." [11] "On the other hand, the father and the master who preside over the family household, which is an imperfect community, have imperfect coercive power." [12] To sum up, the state is, to a degree encountered in almost no other instance, the representative of the "social whole," of "us."

But to get back to our question. How are we to proclaim the inalienability of the individual's rights vis à vis the state if, on the other hand, it is true that in the relationships characteristic of *iustitia distributiva* nothing is due to the individual which is exclusively his? First of all, let us briefly consider the special nature of this kind of obligation. The objection presumably refers first and foremost to the right to life, health and freedom. In what respect is there a special form of obligation in the relationship between individual and state? In his relation to the state, the individual's right to life and health, for example, is not so exclusively his that the state might not require it in the interest of the common good. Against any individual, I may in an emergency defend my life, health, freedom, even my property, to the extent of killing the aggressor. Public authority, however, can quite legitimately deprive an individual of his freedom, not only when he has committed a crime, but also when it so happens that through no fault of his he has fallen victim to a contagious disease that would endanger the social whole. And the administrator of the *bonum commune* can even make decrees affecting the individual's property under certain conditions.

All this does not in any sense imply that the authority of the state must first "endorse" life, freedom and property for the individual, nor that it can grant them to him. Yet, no matter how the powers of public authority are constituted and limited, this much at all events is clear: in his relationship with public authority, a *suum* belongs to a private person in a fashion quite different from that applying to his relations to another private person. It is this peculiar structure in the actual fabric of communal life that we bring to light when we get to the roots of the distinction between commutative justice and distributive justice.

Is there not, then, something "inalienable," as it were, in the individual's rights over and against the social whole? Yes, there is. Wherein does it manifest itself? It is revealed in the limitations and conditions set for these encroachments of the state's authority: that power can only be wielded "*if* the common good demands it." As a member of the whole, the individual has an inalienable right to expect that the distribution of goods, as well as of burdens, be effected justly (i.e., justly in the manner of *iustitia distributiva*). But is there any way to render the individual's inalienable rights secure? Is there any effective way to defend them?

At this point we shall have to speak of another peculiarity of *iustitia distributiva*. We are in the habit of saying that the distinguishing mark of an obligation in the realm of justice is that it is possible to compel its execution. The fulfillment of *iustitia distributiva*, however, cannot be enforced. It is inherent in the concept that no such enforcement should be possible. For who, indeed, is to compel the man in public authority to give the individual what is due to him? Yet it is to him, as the person invested with the state's authority, that distributive justice extends its claims: he is the subject of this particular form of justice. We have here the instance of a person under a definite obligation to grant something that is due to an individual, to give people their "just due," and who yet cannot be compelled to do so. There is no question but that in this instance the inalienability of an individual's rights, which continues to obtain, takes on a very special hue.

If an individual cannot come to some agreement with his neighbor, for instance in the question of settling a debt, both can bring the matter before a third authority, before a court of law. But if a person feels he has not obtained his due from the public authority, there is no "impartial" authority before whom he may bring the matter. But are not "appeal" and "review" possible in the case of an unjust judgment in a court of law? Here we must endeavor to see clearly what this recourse from one authority to the next really means. The highest courts of law, like the lower courts, are organs of but one and the same juridical society. Even the highest tribunal examines nothing but the legal aspects of a case and the application of existing laws. But what if the laws themselves are unjust? What if injustice befalls an individual on the basis of existing laws, simply because he belongs to a certain race, class or religious community? This would be a case in point. To whom, then, could an "appeal" be addressed? Not to mention situations which do not even allow the opportunity for an objection, as, for instance, in the case of an enemy attack, when of necessity the most far-reaching measures may interfere with private rights.

In view of the objective injustice of certain laws, directives, decrees and orders, the question naturally arises concerning the rights of resistance and non-observance, yet never in such a form that the individual affected by those laws and regulations could appear jointly with their author before the tribunal of an independent, superior party equipped with compulsory power. In short, the person invested with the authority of the state, the man who is the subject of *iustitia distributiva*, cannot actually be compelled to the just performance of his office because he himself is at one and the same time guardian and executor of distributive justice. "A ruler is installed for the purpose of guarding justice." [13] "The purpose of power is to realize justice." [14] What if the guardian of justice nevertheless does *not* guard it? Well, then, alas, there

73

is the reign of injustice. And no appeal to any abstract arbiter such as "the conscience of mankind," "the eye of the world," and "the judgment of history" can in any way change it.

Whoever thoroughly examines the structure of *iustitia distributiva* must come to realize very clearly the nature of genuine authority, and to see that no worse or more desperate mishap can be imagined in the world of men than unjust government. And since institutional precautions and controls could entirely prevent the abuse of power only by precluding any form of effective authority, there is nothing and no one that can restrain the man of power from doing injustice,—if not his own sense of justice. In the affairs of the world, everything depends on the rulers' being just.

We have already said that the traditional doctrine of justice is concerned not with the claimant, but with the man owing a claim. It is not concerned with the declaration of human rights, belonging to men as their legitimate claim. Rather, it is the proclamation and establishment of the obligation to respect rights.[15] We are not saying this at this juncture merely for the sake of moralizing. What we have in mind has quite a different significance. At first glance it seems to be a much more aggressive approach to declare rights than to proclaim and establish duties. In reality, quite the

74

reverse is the case. Is not the declaration of a claim by the one entitled to it more of a defensive gesture? A gesture based on a kind of resignation (perhaps a not unfounded one) to the fact that the men under obligation would not concede what is due unless the claimant backed up his demands by force? Reference to the *obligation* in justice, on the other hand, is not only more audacious, but far more realistic as well— all appearances to the contrary. Reference here, to be sure, is not used as a rhetorical term. It is meant to designate the convincing proof of the ground upon which such an obligation rests, and in particular whatever might serve, in the broadest sense, the realization of justice as a human virtue in the state. This approach, therefore, is far more realistic because in the final reckoning it will only be through justice that each man will be given the share that is his, through the justice of those who can give or deny what is due to men; because merely asserting rights never creates justice; because justice in distribution will only be realized through just government. If, however, it is a Utopian dream to think that just government can exist in the world, if it is a Utopian goal to think that the educative efforts of a people should primarily aim at forming the young generation, especially those called to leadership, into just men—then all hope must indeed be abandoned.

One thing, of course, is indispensable: that a sense of the greatness and dignity of governing and ruling [16] be revived in the mind of the public. This is all the more necessary since the "intellectuals" of the past hundred years have been virtually defined by their ironical treatment of the terms "authority" and "subject," with the result that nowadays these words can hardly be spoken or understood without bias. Individualistic Liberalism is in fundamental agreement with orthodox Marxism on this point, namely that there is no "governmental authority" properly so-called. For Individualism, authority is vested in agreements between individuals which, as a matter of principle, can be cancelled at any time; for Marxism, it is the hallmark of those preliminary stages of society which will one day dissolve altogether within a Communistic society.[17]

In his *Politics* [18] Aristotle has raised the question whether or not being a good citizen and a good man are one and the same thing. Can a person who is not a good man nonetheless be a good citizen in the *polis?* He leaves the question in abeyance. On the one hand, he says, a state cannot possibly be composed of nothing but excellent men, and nevertheless there are excellent states. On the other hand, there are states (and they are not the just states) wherein a person can be one of the better and more desirable citizens without being a good man.[19] We are struck by the timeliness of this thought. Aristotle adds a reflective statement which is of interest to us here. He says: there is, perhaps, *one* citizen who is required to be a good man also (i.e., good as man, a man wholly and entirely in order) and that man is the ruler. And on the other hand: the just ruler—according to Bias' maxim that mastery reveals the man [20]—has always been considered as a pre-eminently excellent representative of human virtue, as a man who by the justice of his rule proves that he has resisted those superhuman temptations which assail only the men in authority.

In his treatise on political government [21] Thomas asks about the suitable reward a just king can expect to receive, "since the king's duty to seek the people's good may seem too onerous a task, unless something good accrues to him for himself. It is worth contemplating, then, just what kind of suitable reward there is for a good king." Wealth, honor and renown are mentioned,[22] but all of them put together are considered an inadequate recompense. And when Thomas concludes this magnificent passage with the statement that the just ruler will, "as his reward, be near God and stand at His side inasmuch as he has faithfully exercised the king's divine office over his people," [23] it means that he apportions to the good ruler an incomparable, almost metaphysical distinction of

77

rank, not by virtue of the religious character of his consecration, but on the grounds of his just rule. This view is further strengthened by the words then added: "Even pagan peoples had some prophetic presentiment of this when they believed the leaders and guardians of the people would be transformed into gods." It is more than arbitrary "poetic" allegory when, in his *Divine Comedy*, Dante sees the just kings in the constellation Aquila, fashioned in the shape of an eagle by the lights of those rulers who had been taken up into heaven.[24]

Such formulations are misunderstood if they are interpreted romantically. They are actually based on a highly realistic insight into the danger that usually threatens the ruler, and into the almost superhuman difficulty involved in making *iustitia distributiva* a reality.

If political life is to regain its dignity, a proper appreciation of the eminence of the ruler's task and of the lofty human qualities required for it must be revived in the mind of the public. This means the very opposite of a totalitarian glorification of power. It implies rather that an arduous and unremitting effort of education should impart to the people an incontrovertible ideal image of the requirements a man must meet if he is to exercise authority. It should, for example, be perfectly clear and self-evident to the simplest kind of thinking that wherever prudence and justice are lacking, there can be no fitness for the proper exercise of power. In Aristotle's *Politics*,[25] as well as in the *Summa Theologica* of Thomas Aquinas,[26] these two cardinal virtues are called the virtues characteristic of sovereigns and rulers. Yet according to the moral doctrine of the West the prudent man is certainly not merely a "tactician" able to steer an affair successfully to its conclusion. Prudence implies the kind of objectivity that lets itself be determined by reality, by insight into the facts. He is prudent who can listen in silence, who can take advice so as to gain a more precise, clear and complete knowledge of the facts. If such a standard were applied, it would probably mean that even without formally rejecting him—in fact *before* there were any discussion about him—a rash, brash person, motivated by emotion or craving for power, would *eo ipso* be excluded from running for office, as manifestly unfit to realize the justice of rulers, *iustitia distributiva*. For exercising this justice means, on the one hand, taking the common good into consideration and, on the other, respecting at the same time the dignity of the individual and giving him what is his due.

Up to this point we have spoken of the "ruler" or "king" as the administrator of the common good. In respect to contemporary conditions, our terminology, of course, needs to be corrected and made more precise. But even though there is no occasion in this present context to treat the different forms of government in detail, it may still be noted in passing that according to Thomas Aquinas, monarchy is the form of government which of its very nature most readily guarantees sensible administration of the common good. He also says, however, that of all the possible ways in which authority may degenerate, *unjust* monarchy is the worst. "Just as kingly rule is the best, so is the rule of the tyrant the worst." [27] And there is still another astonishing remark of St. Thomas to consider, namely that tyranny arises more easily and frequently from democracy than from the rule of kings.[28]

In a modern democracy, then, who is the subject of *iustitia distributiva?* The chosen representatives and delegates of the people are the direct subjects; indirectly the voters are. In this connection we should remember that voters are hardly ever active directly as single individuals, but are organized into parties which (as suitable machinery for forming opinion) both name the representatives to be elected and formulate their concrete political aims. The distinctive peculiarity of the democratic form of government as compared with monarchy consists above all—apart from the short period for which the delegate is appointed—in the fact that the representative of the social whole is to a much greater extent the representa-

tive of particular groups or interests as well. Therefore, if ruling is tantamount to administering the
general good of everyone (a notion which is formally denied, for instance, in a concept like the "Dictatorship of the Proletariat" [29]), then the way in
which democracy functions imposes the following
tremendous moral burden upon the individuals, voters
and delegates alike: the individual is obligated by an
ideal image of just distribution without ceasing to be
interested in his own particular right. The main problem facing modern party-democracy is: How can a
party still be impartial? I would not say it is impossible. Indeed, any inconsidered polemic against party
politics as such is highly unrealistic and for that reason irresponsible. Yet we must see that a real problem
and a very specific danger do exist here—or rather, a
task, namely the task of educating men to *iustitia distributiva*.

In this field there are several classic cases of failure.
The following example dates from the last years of
the Weimar Republic: In one of the great wage dis-
putes of that time, the two parties involved in the
dispute appealed to the decision of the federal minister of labor, as a final tribunal. Whereupon this man
who in his role of minister and arbitrator was under
a twofold obligation to the *bonum commune*, declared
that in this case he was primarily secretary of the

trade unions and only secondarily a member of the federal government.[30]

Here the limitations of democracy as a form of government, i.e., as a ministering of the common good, come to light. The limit is reached when it can no longer be expected of an individual that he place the *bonum commune* above his own particular interest. It is not possible, I believe, to determine that precise limit once and for all. Historically speaking there is very considerable scope for variation in terms of the level a people's political education has attained. Thus, in one instance democracy as a government actually exercised jointly by everyone in the community does "work"; in another case it does not.[31] Yet it seems that there are certain boundaries beyond which it cannot be expected from human frailty that concern for the welfare of the whole should overrule the individual's immediate concern or the interest of a special group; these boundaries seem to set limits for democracy as well. There can be small doubt, for instance, that in a "first ballot," the average person cannot be expected to answer the question: "Do you want a higher wage or not?" with the *bonum commune* primarily in view.

Thus, the question: Who actually realizes *iustitia distributiva?* does not always receive a full answer. Thomas says that it is primarily the one who administers the *bonum commune;* but the individual, the "subject" (*subditus*), is also called to the realization of the ideal image of distributive justice; he, too, can be just in the manner of *iustitia distributiva*—indeed, he must be so, if the challenge of the virtue of justice is to be satisfied. Thomas, however, is not speaking here of the individual as participating in the shaping of the common good as voter or delegate; he is thinking of the individual in his capacity as tax payer, for example, or as the man subject to military service, as "the governed," in brief. But how can the individual, from that point of view, still be considered to be a subject of distributive justice, since he has not the slightest chance of "distributing" anything? Thomas gives the following answer: "The act of distributing the goods of the community belongs to none but those who exercise authority over those goods; and yet distributive justice is also in the subjects (*in subditis*) to whom these goods are distributed, insofar as they are contented by a just distribution." [32] This "contentment on the part of the ruled" should not be interpreted as stolidity. It is part of the act of justice to give one's conscious consent to the just and equitable decrees of a political authority acting in the interest of the common good—and not just lip service, but, rather, a consent that molds the actual attitude and conduct. Through his act of consenting, the "subject" takes part in the ruler's justice.

Such a premise does not exclude a legitimate right

to criticism and "opposition." (In fact, Thomas is even of the opinion that laws which do not serve the true common good do not possess any binding power.[33]) It does, however, oppose a biased, negative attitude, illoyal from the very start. Unwarranted criticism and opposition, blind abuse and fault-finding, are acts of injustice, violations of *iustitia distributiva* which alone enables states to exist and function in orderly fashion. Once again it is clear that we are here touching upon a danger inherent in the democratic form of government. Once more we come to a point which calls for rigorous political self-discipline. We are reminded of the words of Donoso Cortes, in a parliamentary address of 1850 concerning the European situation: "The evil that confronts our time is that those who are ruled no longer are willing to be ruled." [34] At this juncture the parliamentary record comments: "Laughter." Donoso Cortes wanted to imply that genuine authority not only requires men fitted for the offices of government, but also presupposes an inner disposition on the part of the governed, a readiness to participate in the just rule by giving their consent to a just administering of the *bonum commune*.

Exactly *what* is distributed in the act of *iustitia distributiva?* We have already quoted the following text from the *Summa Theologica:* In distributive justice something is given to a private individual insofar as what belongs to the whole is due to the part." [35] This means that the share in the *bonum commune* due to the individual is "distributed" to him.

This is the place, then, to seek a somewhat clearer understanding of the concept of "*bonum commune*." Provisionally, the *bonum commune* might be defined as follows: it is the "social product," the total product of community life. The element of truth in this answer is that individuals do work together in all the group activities and professions within a society and cooperate in the production of something that is quite unique, and perhaps irreducible to organized concepts. The result is that food, clothing, shelter, means of communication, transmission of news, care of the sick, education and schools, along with many other kinds of goods for consumption are now available for the people, i.e., the "social whole." The concept *iustitia distributiva* would mean that all these goods are shared and "distributed" in like manner to all members of the community.

One remark: the concepts of "class," "class dispute" and "class struggle" have their place within this context. There is no compelling reason why any Western theory of society should ignore these notions. For the idea of "class dispute" is not to be considered as purely negative. The implication is rather: [36] if one social segment, i.e., a considerable group of the people, considers the prevailing method of sharing the total social product as detrimental to its own legitimate interests and opposes it, therefore, as contrary to the spirit of true communal life, then that social group has become a "class." This attack against the prevailing order generates automatically the resistance of that strata of the society which is interested in maintaining the *status quo* and will therefore defend it. This defense again leads automatically to the formation of another "class." Class dispute, therefore, is the natural result of the existence of various classes within a society. And it is quite conceivable that there might be a class dispute animated by a desire for justice.[37] A totally different meaning attaches to the term "class struggle" in orthodox Marxism. Here, class struggles strive to annihilate the opposing class and to destroy order in a nation. Fruitful dispute among classes, on the contrary, which aims at the "deproletarianizing of the proletariate," not only does not abolish order in the nation (though it may be in constant danger of deteriorating into class struggle), but actually has that order as its goal.

I said above that provisionally we might try to define the concept "*bonum commune*" as the total social product. Yet this definition is still not quite adequate. First of all, it originates in the mental outlook of our technological age which tends to see the true end of society in the techniques of production; in view of its origin, such a definition harbors the danger of obscuring the fact that the *bonum commune* extends far beyond the range of material goods produced by mechanical means. There are contributions to the common weal which, though not immediately "useful," are still indispensable—and of very real value, as well. This is no doubt the sense in which St. Thomas' text is to be understood: The perfection of the human community demands that there be men who dedicate themselves to a life of contemplation,[38] a tenet which signifies that the society of men relies for its functioning on a knowledge of the truth, and that nations thrive in proportion to the depth of reality opened up and accessible to them.

Parenthetically speaking, it becomes possible at this point to formulate a preliminary definition of the totalitarian labor state. It belongs to the principle of such a state that the common good is equated with "common utility." Its projects for the realization of the *bonum commune* are exclusively concerned with utilitarian ends.

A second objection to the definition: The *bonum commune* is the social product, strikes at a much more basic inadequacy. By virtue of the original and enduring meaning of the term *bonum commune*, it represents *the good* (the very essence of those good things) for the sake of which a community exists, and which it must attain and make a reality if it is to be said that all its potentialities have been brought to fruition. For this very reason it appears impossible to give a truly exhaustive, definitive definition of the *bonum commune;* for no one can state with complete finality what the potentialities of the human community are, what the human community "fundamentally" is. No one can give a truly exhaustive account of what man himself "fundamentally" is, and consequently it is just as impossible to give an exhaustive account of everything contained in man's "good," for the sake of which man exists and which he has to realize in his life if it is to be said of him that all his potentialities have been brought to fruition. This and nothing else is the meaning behind the assertion so stubbornly defended by Socrates: That he did not know what "human virtue" was and that he had still to meet the man who knew better.

If we are thus to understand *bonum commune,* what do we mean when we say that we give a man that share in the common good which is due to him? What does it mean to realize *iustitia distributiva?* It means to let individual members of a nation share in the realization of a *bonum commune* that cannot be definitively delineated in concrete terms. Taking part in the realization of that good in accordance with the measure of *dignitas*, capacity and ability that is distinctively his, this is the share which "is due to" the individual and which cannot be withheld from him by the person administering the *bonum commune*, without violating *iustitia distributiva*, the justice proper to rulers. This suggests a much wider reference, namely, that all the good things bestowed in creation (men's capacities and abilities) belong to the "good of the community," and that *iustitia distributiva* entails the obligation of granting such abilities the protection, support and fostering they need.

With this it becomes possible to formulate one more essential element of totalitarian government. The person endowed with political power claims to give a comprehensive definition of the tangible content of the *bonum commune*. The fact that a "five-year-plan" tries to achieve a higher rate of industrial production or seeks a closer adjustment between supply and demand is not in itself a fatally destructive feature. Fatally destructive is the elevation of such a "plan" to an exclusive standard to which not only the production of goods is subordinated but also the work at the universities, the creative activity of the artist, and the use of leisure. Thus, everything that cannot be justified by this standard must, for that simple reason, suffer suppression as "socially unimportant" and "undesirable."

It is in the nature of things that a "distributor" should take some thought of the person who receives, but that a "buyer" should consider only the actual objective value of the thing received. Here we are faced, as has already been said, with the main distinction between *iustitia distributiva* and commutative justice. In fulfilling the justice of government the administrator of the *bonum commune* necessarily considers the person and his *dignitas* (dignity can, in this case, signify both a special aptitude for a certain office and "worthiness" [in the proper sense] i.e., meritorious service distinguished by public recognition). It seems to me that, generally speaking, few things appear to point so patently to the inner corruption of political community life as the sceptical or cynical indifference with which the young generation of today looks upon distinctions bestowed by the state. There may well be valid reason for such scepticism, yet we cannot overlook how disturbingly it reveals the lack of confidence in the fundamental function of the ruler's justice, the act of "distributing." But that is a fresh theme.

At present, however, the main point at issue is the peculiar structure of the act of distributing and, more especially, respect for the person (*acceptio personarum*) and for his *dignitas*. There are clearly two distinct ways in which we can have respect for a person. One way looks to the person with the aim of effecting just equality; through the other, such equality is completely frustrated. This is the distinction between impartial and partial respect for the person. In the present instance impartial respect is seen to be the specific requirement of distributive justice, partiality its specific ruin.[39]

A moment's thought will show that one of the most easily recognizable characteristics of the contemporary totalitarian constellation of power is expressly to cast suspicion on impartiality and objectivity, while it is part of its program to declare that partiality and "following the party line" constitute the very essence of true public spirit. Such maxims must be considered a threat and temptation to men's political thinking throughout the whole world. They should help us to realize the urgency for restoring in the public's mind the idea of justice as it is formulated in traditional doctrine and contained in the old-fashioned Biblical formula, "respect for the person" (*acceptio personarum*). That expression recurs constantly in both the Old and New Testaments. "Judge that which is just, whether he be of your own country, or a stranger. You shall hear the little as well as the great: neither shall you respect any man's person: because it is the judgment of God." This statement is made in the Book of Deuteronomy (I, 16 ff) on the direction of Moses to the overseers and judges. In the New Testament, in one of Paul's Epistles (Eph. 6, 9), the admonition (likewise directed to the "lords") is found: "Thou knowest that the Lord both of them and you (slaves) is in heaven: and there is no respect of persons with him."

Thomas has devoted a special question to this notion.[40] "It is respect of persons when something is allotted to a person out of proportion to his deserts" (*praeter proportionem dignitatis ipsius*).[41] The typical instance of "respect of persons," and the one which threatens political communal life, is not so much the case in which a man receives (or does not receive) distinction and honor at variance with his true merit. It is rather that public offices and administrative positions are conferred upon men without concern for their qualifications. The *Summa Theologica* sets down in incontrovertible terms what impartial regard for the person and unjust "respect of persons" is. "If you promote a man," Thomas writes,[42] "to a professorship on account of his having sufficient knowledge, you consider the due cause, not the person"—though the candidate must still be examined very thoroughly and hence, "looked over" very carefully. "But if, in conferring something or someone, you consider in him not the fact that what you give him is proportionate or due to him, but the fact that he is this particular man, Peter or Martin, then there is respect of the person." Or, "if a man promote someone to a prelacy or a professorship because he is rich or because he is a relative of his, it is respect of persons." [43] For the rest, however, Thomas showed realistic restraint in leaving to experience the wholly independent matter of establishing the precise qualifications and merits actually required for a certain post. This refraining from assertion here is part of the matter in hand. Wishing to define a suitable qualification abstractly and "in itself," *simpliciter et secundum se*, is not feasible. Thus a case is quite conceivable in which (in a religious office, for example) a man who is less holy and learned may nevertheless make a greater contribution to the common good—perhaps by virtue of his greater capacity for successfully completing a project or because of his "worldly" industry.[44] The same practical wisdom expressed in this remark is repeated in a book on friendship by the Cistercian abbot, Aelred of Rievaux, in which he says offices must not be bestowed for any reason other than qualifications; for even Christ did not make his favorite disciple, John, the head of His Church.[45]

It is left, then, to *prudentia regnativa*, the prudence of the ruler, and distributive justice to recognize true "worthiness" and to distribute offices and honors in due proportion to real *dignitas*. That means preserving and realizing the equality of justice in spite of having respect for persons; for equality will be just as surely violated by respect of persons as it will be by an indiscriminate treatment of everyone which systematically overlooks any and all distinctions.

Justly combining a viewpoint which looks to men's distinctive qualifications and merits with a point of view that considers men's natural equality (for there certainly is a proper worth which is *in the same proportion* in *every* man who bears the countenance of man!) is an almost impossible task. We might say that in this case more than human effort is required. Here we stand in real need of the "favor of the fates" and "the favorable dispensation" of superhuman powers. In a work of Plato's [46] old age there is a passage that expresses this point in memorable fashion. Above all else, Plato says, the statesman must constantly keep in mind that justice in virtue of which everyone, though possessed of unequal abilities, receives his due in proportion to his right. But from time to time, so that internal discord within the state may be averted, it is inevitable that equality—"so-called" equality, as Plato terms it—take the place of justice. Occasionally, then, the statesman must make use of the equality of the fates. Yet in so doing he should not neglect to appeal to "God and good fortune," praying that they may let the die fall in the way that is most just. What portion of irony, of helplessness, and again of trust in the dispensation of the gods are contained in this Platonic thought—who can tell?

VII. THE LIMITS OF JUSTICE

WE HAVE ALREADY said that it is of the nature of communal life for men constantly to become indebted to each other and then just as constantly paying one another the debt. We have further said that as a result the balance is in a constant state of shift and needs constantly to be restored to equilibrium. The act of justice is precisely to effect this process of compensations, restitutions and satisfactions for debts.

It now remains for us to state that the world cannot be kept in order through justice alone. The condition of the historical world is such that the balance cannot always be fully restored through restitution and the paying of debts and dues. The fact that some debts are not or cannot be paid is essential to the world's actual condition. Now there are two aspects to this situation.

Firstly: there are some obligations which, by their very nature, cannot be acquitted in full, much as the one who is thus indebted may be willing to do so. And as justice means to give a person what is due to him, *debitum reddere*, this signifies that there exist relations of indebtedness beyond the scope of the realization of justice. On the other hand, the very relationships which are characterized by this disparity are also the ones fundamental for human existence. And it is naturally the just man, i.e., the man who has a firm and constant will to give each man what is his, who will experience that incontrovertible disparity with special acuteness.

It becomes immediately clear that what is meant here is first and foremost man's relation to God. "Whatever man renders to God is due, yet it cannot be equal, as though man rendered to God as much as he owes Him!" [1] This statement is not to be understood as if man were a mere nonentity before God. In a certain sense, Thomas says, something does belong to him, something is "due" to him, which God does give to man. Something belongs to man "by reason of his nature and condition." [2] It is also true that man's nature is created, that is to say, it has not come into existence by reason of anything other than God Himself. "Now the work of divine justice always presupposes the work of mercy; and is founded thereon." [3] This must not be taken to be merely an edifying thought. It is a very precise description of man's condition in the face of God. *Before* any subsequent claim is made by men, indeed even before the mere possibility of such a human claim arises, comes the fact that man has been made a gift by God (of his being), such that his nature cannot ever "make it good," discharge it, "deserve" it, or return it again. Man can never say to God: We are even.

This is the way in which *"religion,"* as a human attitude, is connected with justice. Thomas quite naturally speaks of *religio* within the context of his theory of the virtue of justice. The significance of this connection,—and incidentally St. Thomas has been taken to task for making it (the charge being that he "subordinates" religion to one of the acquired virtues)— the significance of this connection is that the inner structure of religious acts first becomes intelligible when man, by reason of his relations with God, has recognized in the disparity between himself and God something which simply cannot be obliterated, a disparity consisting in the fact that a *debitum* exists which his nature cannot repay by any human effort, no matter how heroic it may be, a disparity which simply cannot be overcome. Perhaps it might be possible for contemporary man to gain a view of the reality and significance of *sacrifice* in the cult as a fundamental religious act if he approached it by this rarely travelled path—via the concept of justice, of restitution of something due. From this perspective, it is more easily understood why the offering of sacrifice should be a requirement of justice linked to man's condition as *creatura*. Thomas has actually formulated this point:

Oblatio sacrificii pertinet ad ius naturale,[4] the obligation of sacrifice is an obligation of natural law. I claim that this doctrine is more easily understood if we set out with the idea of a *debitum* that cannot be repaid, i.e., with the notion of an actually existing obligation that nevertheless and by its very nature cannot be wiped out. Here perhaps is the key to the extravagance inherent in religious acts. Helplessness and impotency prompt this extravagance; because it is impossible to do what "properly" ought to be done, an effort beyond the bounds of reason, as it were, tries to compensate for the insufficiency. This explains the excesses of sacrificial offerings such as self-annihilation, killing, burning. Socrates, in the *Gorgias*, says with a most unclassical and indeed an almost unaccountable recklessness (which it would be wrong to interpret simply as an ironical paradox) that a person who has committed injustice must scourge himself, allow himself to be imprisoned, go into exile, accept execution, and yet with all that be the first one to accuse himself, "so that he might be freed from the greatest of evils, from injustice." [5] Here, the old Athenian, who pursued justice with such relentless ardor, speaks from the very same assumption which prompts the doctors of Western Christendom to speak of an *excessus poenitentiae*, an excess proper to the true spirit of penance. In the *Summa Theologica* Thomas formulates the following objection (and it is his answer to this objection which is important to us at this point): The spirit of penance and the spirit of justice are utterly different in that justice clings to the reasonable mean, whereas penance actually consists in an *excessus*. This is his answer to that problem. In certain fundamental relations, for example in man's relation to God, the equality that properly belongs to the concept of justice, i.e., equality between debt and payment, cannot be achieved. Therefore, the one who is in debt strives to pay back whatever is in his power to remit. "Yet this will not be sufficient simply (*simpliciter*). But only according to the acceptance of the higher one, and this is what is meant by ascribing excess to penance," *hoc significatur per excessum, qui attribuitur poenitentiae.*[6] Such *excessus*, then, seems to be a quality of every properly religious act, of sacrifice, adoration and devotion. It is an attempt to respond to the fact of a relation of indebtedness, an attempt that is the most "adequate" possible under the circumstances, but one that must always remain "inadequate" because it cannot ever achieve a complete *restitutio*. At this point it becomes possible to see why "justice" in the realm of religion can even be perversity, as man boasts of the restitution he makes: "I fast twice in a week. I give tithes of all that I possess" (*Luke* 18, 12). The true attitude is, rather: "So you also, when you shall have done all these things that are commanded you, say: we are unprofitable servants" (*Luke* 17, 10).

Thomas speaks of *pietas* as well as of religion. This is a term which cannot be rendered with complete accuracy by our derivation "piety"; and in the discussion which follows it must be remembered that the same applies wherever, for want of a more precise rendering, we have to use the anglicized term. Piety, too, depends on something being due a person which of its very nature cannot be fully repaid. Piety, likewise, is a tendency of the soul which can be fully realized only if man sees himself as the partner in an obligation which can never be truly and fully acquitted, no matter how great the counter-service rendered. "Piety" applies to the parent-child relationship. "It is not possible to make to one's parents an equal return of what one owes to them; and thus piety is annexed to justice." [7] This link indicates that only the just man, in his persistent effort to effect a balance between debts and payments, truly experiences the impossibility of full restitution and "takes it to heart." Piety presupposes the virtue of justice.

Should we set ourselves the task of re-establishing piety as an integral part of the ideal image of man (for it must be frankly admitted that piety is no longer considered a quality necessary to man's "righteousness," nor its lack as indicative of man's inner disorder), the first step would have to be to restore this assumption: that the relation of children to parents might be experienced by the children as an obligation beyond the scope of full restitution. In a word, familial order would have to be restored—in actual fact and in people's estimation. Of course, "familial order" embraces more than the relation between parents and children; but unless it is restored, we cannot expect that the inner experience of an unrepayable obligation should bear as its fruit the feeling of piety.

In speaking of piety, Thomas does not confine himself to the relation between parent and child; he includes man's relation to his country as well. "Man is debtor chiefly to his parents and his country, after God. Wherefore, just as it belongs to religion to give worship to God, so does it belong to piety to give worship to one's parents and one's country." [8] Here we meet with a considerable difficulty. No matter how wide the scope within which we comprise our obligations to our people—counting as goods the language with its inexhaustible treasure of wisdom; the protection afforded by law and order; the participation in whatever can be thought of as the "common good" of a people—yet it remains supremely difficult to accept the thought that it belongs to the image of full and true humanity "to show reverence to one's country," *cultum exhibere patriae.* And as we realize, on further thought, that this difficulty cannot be overcome simply by resolution, that what is implied here goes infinitely beyond the irreverence or the ill-will or the illoyalty of the individual, we begin to measure the extent of the deterioration in the ideal image of man and man's communal life in Western civilization.

This comes into even clearer focus in the third concept Thomas mentions alongside *religio* and *pietas*. It is a concept equally concerned with man's reaction to a condition wherein a debt cannot be cancelled. It is the concept of "respect," of *observantia*. The fact that this term has dropped out of current usage, that we have no precise, contemporary equivalent for it, indicates sufficiently that the concept itself has become foreign to us. What, then, does *observantia* mean?

Observantia indicates the respect we feel inwardly and express outwardly toward those persons who are distinguished by their office or by some dignity.[9] We have only to lend an ear to the ironic overtones currently connected with the words "dignity" and "office" to realize at once how remote from us is the reality which Western moral theory has formulated in the concept *observantia* and made an integral part of the ideal image of the ordered man and the ordered community. That theory states that no man can give a recompense equivalent to *virtus* [10]—*virtus* meaning, in this instance, the ability or power (both moral and intellectual) of rightly administering an office. Consequently, a situation arises in which the individual cannot adequately satisfy an obligation. The individual, in his private existence, profits from the proper administration of public offices—by the judge, the teacher, and the like.[11] These men and women create a well-ordered communal life. For this, the individual finds himself indebted to the holders of such offices, in a fashion which cannot be acquitted fully by "payment." It is this situation which is acknowledged by the "respect" shown a person holding an office of public responsibility. The objection that irresponsible and inefficient men may hold offices is of little weight. Thomas' answer is that the office and, in a more general sense, the community as a whole are honored in the person who holds the office.[12]

The root of the matter is here evidently a conception of man which takes the interdependence of individuals for granted and sees in it nothing shameful or detrimental to the dignity of the person.[13] In any event, within the reality of the world, an ordered community life without leadership and, therefore, without "dependence," is unthinkable. And that holds true of the family as well as of the state—and for the state that is democratically constituted as well as for a dictatorship. Generally speaking, a certain formal structure remains in force at all times and in all places; and if it is not realized in the right way, then it is realized in the wrong way. So that the question can arise whether the void created by the disappearance of the notion of *observantia* (a process certainly not due, however, to mere whim and wilfullness) may not have permitted the establishment of another form of relation between superior and subordinate: the shameful expression of mutual contempt which our current jargon renders in the terms "bossing" and "bossed."

This, then, is one aspect of the fact that the world is not to be kept in order through justice alone. There are obligations and debts which of their very nature cannot be adequately fulfilled and discharged. Only the just man takes pains to give each man his due, and only the just man, accordingly, fully experiences that disparity and undertakes to overcome it by some kind of "excess." He fulfills the *debitum* in the clear knowledge that he will never quite succeed in acquitting himself in full measure. For that reason the element of rationality so proper to justice is linked so closely with the exaggeration and, as it were, inadequacy which characterize *religio*, *pietas* and *observantia*. All three of these concepts are, therefore, an abomination for rational thought.

Now we can map out a second way of interpreting the proposition of the "limits" of justice. The proposition, in fact, would come to mean that in order to keep the world going, we must be prepared to give what is not in the strictest sense obligatory (whereas, let us remember, the first interpretation of the same proposition was that there are obligations in the strictest sense of the term which man is nonetheless incapable of fulfilling).

The just man, who has a more keenly felt experience of these first inadequacies the more fully he realizes that his very being is a gift, and that he is heavily indebted before God and man, is also the man willing to give where there is no strict obligation. He will be willing to give another man something no one can compel him to give. Evidently, there are some actions which one cannot be compelled to perform and which are nonetheless obligatory in the strict sense of the word—telling the truth, for instance. Expressing one's thanks to another is giving him his just due, even though this obviously cannot be enforced. But "being grateful" and "returning thanks" are not of the same order as "paying" and "making restitution." That is why Thomas says, quoting from Seneca, that a person who wants to repay a gift too quickly with a gift in return is an unwilling debtor and an ungrateful person.[14]

So once again, the man who strives for justice, and he above all, realizes (Thomas says) that fulfilling an obligation and doing what he is really obliged to do are not all that is necessary. Something more is required, something over and above, such as liberality, *affabilitas*, kindness, if man's communal life is to remain human. Here nothing more (and certainly nothing *less*) is meant than friendliness in our everyday associations. This "virtue"—and Thomas relates it, too, to justice—is, of course, strictly neither due to another person nor can it be rightfully claimed and demanded. Still it is impossible for men to live together joyfully (*delectabiliter*) without it. "Now as man could not live in society without truth, so likewise not without joy (*delectatio*)." [15]

I can well imagine how the average young man of our day will respond to these ideas. That he may not enter into them with any great enthusiasm is only to be expected. For the harsher and more "realistic" manner of present-day existence is much more congenial to him. And it is true that we can only with difficulty divest ourselves from the influence of the prevailing atmosphere. Still, it is not the traditional doctrine of justice but precisely our present-day atmosphere which is "unrealistic." That is also the reason why it is so difficult to overcome. But perhaps I may venture the suggestion that one should try, without bias or rash preconceptions, simply to listen to the exposition of the ideal image of justice and follow it through to its final consequence. It is not inconceivable that in the process of listening, it might suddenly become clear that the harsher, more "realistic" approach is nothing but a sign of poverty, of the steadily advancing erosion and aridity of interhuman relationships. It might well become plausible that the manifold and

varied forms of partnership of which man is capable
(insofar as he is "just") constitute in fact the riches
of man and of the human community.

Human life will necessarily become inhuman if
man's dues to man are determined by pure calculation.[16] That the just man give to another what is *not*
due to him is particularly important since injustice is
the prevailing condition in our world. Because men
must do without things that are due to them (since
others are withholding them unjustly); since human
need and want persist even though no specific person
fails to fulfill his obligation, and even though no binding obligation can be construed for anyone; for these
very reasons it is not "just and right" for the just man
to restrict himself to rendering only what is strictly
due. For it is true, as Thomas says, that "mercy without justice is the mother of dissolution"; but, also,
that "justice without mercy is cruelty." [17]

Now it becomes possible to state the inner limits
of justice: "To be willing to watch over peace and
harmony among men through the commandments of
justice is not enough when charity has not taken firm
root among them." [18]

NOTES

In the following notes, quotations from the *Summa Theologica* of St. Thomas Aquinas, are indicated only by ciphers; "II, II, 58, 2 ad 4" stands for *Summa Theologica*, 2nd part of the 2nd part, question 58, article 2, answer to the 4th objection. The same applies to quotations from his *Commentary on the Book of the Sentences of Peter Lombard;* "2. d. 24, 3, 5" stands for 2nd book, distinction 24, question 3, article 5. Titles of other works of St. Thomas are abbreviated as follows:

Summa contra Gentes (C.G.)
Quaestio disputata de virtutibus cardinalibus (Virt. Card.)
Quaestio disputata de virtutibus in communi (Virt. comm.)
De regimine principum (Reg. princ.)
Commentary on the Nichomachean Ethics of Aristotle (In Eth.)
Commentary on the Politics of Aristotle (In Pol.)
Commentary on Dionysius the Aeropagite, On the Divine Names (In Div. Nom.)
Commentary on the Gospel of Matthew (In Matth.)
Commentary on the Epistle to the Ephesians (In Ephes.)

I. ON RIGHTS

1. Kant, *Eine Vorlesung über Ethik*, Paul Menzer (2d edition, Berlin 1925), p. 245.
2. Thomas Aquinas, *In Eth.*, 5, 1; No. 893.

3. *Republic* 331.—Plato quotes the poet Simonides who lived over a century earlier than he did. Simonides, however, is not the author of this idea, for it is formulated already in Homer, in the *Odyssey* (14, 84).

4. *Rhetoric* 1, 9.

5. *De finibus* 5, 23.

6. *De officiis* 1, 24.

7. *The City of God* 19, 21.

8. *Corpus Juris Civilis, Instit.* I, 1.

9. II, II, 58, 1.—It is a matter, as Thomas says, of repeating, in the proper form of a definition, the formula encountered in Roman Law.

10. Especially in the *Summa Theologica* (II, II, 57-122) and in the *Commentary on the Nichomachean Ethics of Aristotle* (*In Eth.*, 5; Nos. 885-1108).

11. *Virt. Card.*, I ad 12.

12. *In Div. Nom.*, 8, 4; No. 778.

13. *Patrologia Latina* (Migne), 220, 633.

14. *C.G.* 2, 28.

15. *Ibid.*

16. *Ibid.*

17. *Non igitur creatio ex debito justitiae procedit. C.G.* 2, 28.

18. I, 21, 1 ad 3.

19. II, II, 57, 1.

20. Thomas says in the *Summa Contra Gentes* (2, 93): *Quod ad perfectionem alicujus requiritur* belongs to man, and therefore, those things that a man necessarily has. Need and necessity (*exigentia, necessitas*) are expressed in "belonging to" (I, 21, 1 ad 3). In the once famous book by R. von Ihering, *Der Zweck im Recht*, it is stated: "To have a right means: There is something there for us" Volksausgabe I, p. 49. Emil Brunner (*Gerechtigkeit*, Zurich 1943) speaks of the "order of

rights" into which man finds himself introduced by the idea of justice (p. 22).

21. Plato, *Gorgias* 469.

22. *Ibid.* 508.

23. II, II, 57, 2.

24. II, II, 57, 2 ad 2.

25. We can, of course, in a very improper sense, speak of a person treating an animal "justly" or "unjustly"; we can even say that cruelty to animals is "unjust." Something of the same sort occurs in the usual expression of the "material justice" of an artistic action. In the exact meaning of the word, however, beings that are not spiritual do not have inalienable rights; something cannot properly "belong" to them; they themselves, rather, belong to man.

26. J. Leclerq, "Note sur la justice," *Revue Néoscolastique de Philosophie*, 28th year (1926), p. 269.

27. J.-P. Sartre, *Existentialism*, Philosophical Library (New York 1947) p. 18.

28. *C.G.* 3, 112.

29. *C.G.* 3, 112.

30. *Vorlesung über Ethik*, p. 245.

31. 4 d. 46, 1, 2, 1.

32. Cf. Josef Pieper, *Traktat über die Klugheit* (4th ed., Munich 1950), especially the second chapter "Knowledge of the reality and realization of the good." (*Das Wissen um die Wirklichkeit und die Verwirklichung des Guten.*)

II. DUTY IN RELATION TO "THE OTHER"

1. II, 57, 1.

2. Thomas speaks of *alietas* and *diversitas*: II, II, 58, 2.

3. Of course, there is also a broader notion of justice that does not exclude charity, just as there is also a notion

of charity that includes within itself the notion of
justice.

4. II, II, 58, 2.

5. II, II, 57, 4.

6. In Franz Dornseiff, *Der deutsche Wortschatz* (3rd ed.,
Berlin 1943) the word *"Ohrenbläserei"* (tale bearing)
is assigned to the word-group "flattery" (p. 556).

7. II, II, 74, 2.

8. *Justitia consistit in communicatione. In Eth.* 8, 9; No.
1658.

9. II, II, 102, 2 ad 2.

10. *Dependet ex honestate debentia.* II, II, 106, 4 ad 1.

11. *Inter virtutes morales sola justitia potest Deo magis
proprie attribui. In Div. Nom.,* 8, 4; No. 771.

12. I, 21, 4.

13. *Reddit sibi quod sibi debetur.* I, 21, 1 ad 3.

14. *Proslogion* 10.

15. I, 21, 1 ad 3.

16. *Alteri obligatum esse.* II, II, 122, 1.

17. *Republic* 332.

18. II, II, 122, 1.

19. II, II, 122, 1.

20. II, II, 122, 1, *sed contra.*

21. II, II, 58, 5.

22. Thomas interprets (II, II, 58, 5 ad 3) the text from the
New Testament (I John 3, 4) in the following sense—
every sin is *in-iquitas.*

23. *Virt. card.* 3 ad 8; II, II, 58, 6 ad 4; 79, 1.

24. II, II, 47, 10 ad 1; *In Eth.* 5, 2; No. 907.

25. II, II, 58, 5.

26. *In Eth.* 5, 2; No. 907.

27. *Nichomach. Ethics* 5, 3; 1129b.

28. II, II, 79, 1.

29. *In Eth.* 5, 1; No. 886.

30. *Lecture on Ethics,* p. 245.

31. I, II, 100, 2.
32. *Secundum rationem commensurationis ad alterum.* I, II, 60, 2.
33. 3 d. 33, 2, 1, 3.
34. I, II, 60, 2.
35. Cf. Joseph Pieper, *Fortitude and Temperance* (Pantheon, New York 1954) pp. 61 ff.
36. Commentary on I, II, 60, 2.
37. *Virt. card.* I ad 12.
38. II, II, 122, 1.
39. II, II, 181, 1 ad 1.
40. I, II, 100, 9 ad 1.—It should not go unsaid that this statement is made with regard to the law of the *Old* Covenant. Yet the text that has been quoted is not immediately affected by this restriction.
41. This example is cited by Sertillanges in his *Philosophie Morale de S. Thomas* (Paris 1922), p. 244.
42. *In Eth.* 5, 13; No. 1044.
43. 5, 9 f.
44. I, II, 107, 4.—This statement, once again by way of merely noting the point, was made in a question about the law of the *New* Covenant.
45. II, II, 58, 10.

III. THE RANK OF JUSTICE

1. *De officiis* 1, 7.
2. II, II, 58, 3.
3. Thus writes Ambrose in his *De officiis* (1, 35), a book that is also inspired by Cicero's writing of the same title.
4. *C.G.* 3, 24.
5. *In Eth.* 5, 2; No. 910.
6. I, II, 66, 4.
7. II, II, 58, 12; I, II, 66, 1.
8. *Virt. commun.* 9.

9. I, II, 66, 4.
10. II, II, 124, 1.
11. *Justitia est hujus boni factiva.* II, II, 123, 12.
12. II, II, 157, 4.
13. II, II, 123, 12.
14. II, II, 123, 12.
15. *Per eam (= justitiam) applicatur voluntas ad proprium actum.* I, II, 59, 5.
16. *In Eth.* 5, 15; No. 1077.
17. Plotinus, *Enneads* I, 2, 6: Δικαιοσυνη δε ειπερ δικειοπραγια.
18. II, II, 55, 8.
19. Cf. Josef Pieper, *The End of Time* (Pantheon, New York 1954), the chapter about the figure of Antichrist.

IV. THE BASIC FORMS OF JUSTICE

1. Diogenes Laertius, *Lives and Opinions* I, 36.
2. Plutarch, *Banquet of the Seven Wise Men,* ch. 11.
3. *Reg. princ.* 1, 10.
4. The text is handed on in Aristotle's *Nichomachean Ethics* (5, 3; 1130a).
5. Plutarch, *Banquet,* ch. 11.
6. *Ibid.*
7. Diogenes Laertius, *Lives and Opinions* I, 69.
8. Plutarch, *Banquet,* ch. 11.
9. *Ibid.*
10. II, II, 61, 1.
11. *In Eth.* 1, 1; No. 5.
12. Cf. in addition O. Spann, *Gesellschaftslehre* (3rd ed., Leipzig 1930) p. 157 f.

V. RECOMPENSE AND RESTITUTION

1. I, II, 114, 1.—*Simpliciter . . . justum est inter aequales.* III, 85, 3.

2. 4 d. 46, 1, 1, 1.–cf. *C.G.* 1, 93; 1, 21, 1; *In Div. Nom.* 8, 4; No. 775.
3. *Commutationes, secundum quas transfertur aliquid ab uno in alterum . . . . In Eth.* 5, 4; No. 928.
4. II, II, 61, 3.
5. Cf. Josef Pieper, *Grundformen sozialer Spielregeln* (2nd ed., Frankfurt 1950), particularly the chapter "Die Spielregeln der Gesellschaft."
6. II, II, 62, 1.
7. This is the translation of M. S. Gillet, O.P., in the French-Latin *Summa Theologica* in the Editions de la Revue des Jeunes (Paris-Tournai-Rome 1932); II, II, 61 pro-œmium.
8. II, II, 62, 1.
9. So, for example, B. H. Merkelbach, *Summa Theologiae Moralis* (2nd ed., Paris 1936), II, 284.
10. *Grundlagen der Moral.* Collected Works (Insel ed.), II, p. 611.
11. II, II, 61, 3.
12. II, II, 61, 3.
13. *Per restitutionem fit reductio ad aequalitatem.* II, II, 62, 5.

VI. THE JUSTICE OF GOVERNMENT

1. II, II, 58, 7 ad 2.
2. II, II, 61, 1 ad 5.
3. II, II, 61, 2.
4. I, 21, 1; cf. also *In Eth.* 5, 4; No. 927, 928.
5. II, II, 61, 2.
6. II, II, 61, 2.
7. II, II, 61, 2 ad 2.
8. *In Eth.* 5, 6; No. 950.
9. *Nichomach. Ethics* 5, 7; 1131b.
10. *In Pol.* 1, 1; No. 11.
11. The idea of "mutilation" is not as "medieval" as it may

first appear. Sterilization as a measure of punishment exists, for instance, in modern states; and the right to it, as a matter of principle, is not denied even by the Church. Cf., for example, *Lexicon für Theologie und Kirche,* vol. 9, col. 813.

12. II, II, 65, 2 ad 2.
13. *In Eth.* 5, 11; No. 1009.
14. *In Ephes.* 6, 3.
15. This apparently is not true of the West's classical doctrine of justice alone. For Chung-Sho Lo, a professor of philosophy and Chinese member of the Unesco Commission that has prepared the new formulation of human rights, made the point, much to people's embarrassment, that in the Chinese tradition there is no concept of human right and the Chinese language does not possess any word exactly corresponding to our word "right." There is, of course, a notion of "justice" and also a much different doctrine of the justice of the sovereign. To this effect Chung-Sho Lo quoted the *Book of Stories,* a book almost two thousand years old: "Heaven loves the people and the sovereign must obey heaven." Cf. *Um die Erklärung der Menschenrechte* (Zurich 1951), p. 242 ff.
16. Cf. also on this point Romano Guardini, *Die Macht* (Würzburg 1951) p. 91 f.
17. "There will be no longer any proper political power," says K. Marx (*Elend der Philosophie,* Berlin 1952, p. 194).
18. *Pol.* 3, 4; 1276b.
19. On this score Thomas says that in the best state it is not possible to be a good citizen without that capacity in virtue of which a man is a good man. *In Pol.* 3, 3; No. 366; cf. *In Eth.* 5, 3; No. 926.
20. Thomas quotes him as follows: *"Principatus virum ostendit." Reg. princ.* 1, 10.

21. *Reg. princ.* 1, 8.
22. The Commentary on the *Nichomachean Ethics* says, honor and glory are the best things that men may give to the just ruler; naturally, the tyrant wants material gain over and above that. *In Eth.* 5, 11; No. 1011.
23. *Reg. princ.* 1, 10.
24. *Divine Comedy*, Paradiso, canto 18.
25. *Pol.* 3, 4; 1277b.
26. II, II, 50, 1 ad 1.
27. *Reg. princ.* 1, 4.
28. *Reg. princ.* 1, 6.
29. "The proletarian state is a machine for the suppression of the bourgeoisie"; "dictatorship of the proletariat is the government of the proletariat over the bourgeoisie, a government that is restricted by no law and that rests on power." J Stalin, *Über die Grundlagen des Leninismus* (Berlin 1946), p. 30 f.
30. It concerned the iron dispute of the Northwest group and Wissell, the federal minister of labor at that time.
31. Conditions in England, for instance, are undoubtedly different from those in Germany. Yet in this field no settlement is valid once and for all. We must, however, see the point political self-discipline must attain, if a serious settlement is to come into effect.
32. II, II, 61, 1 ad 3.
33. I, II, 96, 6.
34. Donoso Cortes, *Der Abfall vom Abendland*. Dokumente. Published by Paul Viator (Vienna 1948), p. 67.
35. II, II, 61, 2.
36. The next paragraph is a self-quotation from Josef Pieper, *Thesen zur sozialen Politik* (Freiburg 1946), p. 8.
37. Encyclical *Quadragesimo anno*.
38. 4 d. 26, 1, 2.
39. *Opponitur justitiae distributivae.* II, II, 63, prologue.
40. II, II, 63.

41. II, II, 63, 2.
42. II, II, 63, 1.
43. II, II, 63, 1.
44. II, II, 63, 2.
45. Aelred of Rievaux, *On Spiritual Friendship*, III, 4 (PL. 195, 697-698).
46. *Laws* 757.

VII. THE LIMITS OF JUSTICE

1. II, II, 80, 1.
2. I, 21, 1 ad 3.
3. I, 21, 4.
4. II, II, 85, 1.—*All* men, the *Summa Theologica* goes on to say (II, II, 86, 4 ad 2), knew at least implicitly the meaning of sacrifice.
5. *Gorgias* 480.
6. III, 85, 3 ad 2.
7. II, II, 80, 1.
8. II, II, 101, 1.
9. *Personae in dignitate constitutae* (II, II, 102, 1); *personae dignitate praecellentes* (II, II, 103, 3).
10. II, II, 80, 1.
11. In an enumeration that is not intended to be complete, Thomas speaks (II, II, 102, 1) of sovereigns, generals, masters: *et simile est in aliis.*
12. II, II, 103, 2 ad 2.
13. Emil Brunner (*Gerechtigkeit*, p. 50) refers to Rousseau on this score. He (Rousseau) would have the family dissolve itself as soon as cooperation is no longer necessary, so that the children might attain full independence as quickly as possible, that alone being suitable for men.
14. II, II, 106, 4.
15. II, II, 114, 2 ad 1.

16. It is scarcely necessary to go into any details concerning the appalling timeliness of this idea. In a report on his imprisonment (. . . *Und führen wohin Du nicht willst*, 4th ed., Munich 1952; English tr. *Unwilling Journey*, Muhlenberg Press, Philadelphia) H. Gollwitzer, speaking of his own experience, said that "old prisoners" would only let their comrades, who had perhaps become ill, share in their allotted ration in accordance with the output they actually achieved: "They could as little understand our appeal to sympathy and comradeship as we could understand their stubborn calculation of what belonged to each man—a calculation on which the Soviet Union's whole system of living is erected" (p. 101).

17. *In Matth.* 5, 2.

18. C.G. 3, 130.

A Schematic Representation of the Basic Forms
of Justice (cf. p. 52 to p. 55)

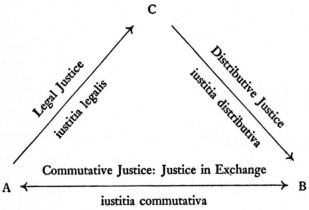

The Social Whole

C

Legal Justice
iustitia legalis

Distributive Justice
iustitia distributiva

Commutative Justice: Justice in Exchange

A ⟷ B

iustitia commutativa

The Individual Person   *The Individual Person*